In following unfamiliar trails leading to distant goals, we may well pause from time to time and take a backward glance. Courage falters if our best efforts seem to bring us no closer to our objective and if instead the road becomes rougher and more uncertain as unsuspected obstacles threaten to check our progress. But as we look back over the distance that lies between our starting point and our present position, we realize that our striving was not in vain, that we have moved forward in spite of all impediments and have overcome difficulties once considered insuperable.

Such a retrospective glance is especially useful in the field of psychiatry. The magnitude of the efforts to be expended on our task, the impenetrable darkness that hides the innermost workings of the brain and their relation to psychic manifestations, and finally the inadequacy of our instruments for dealing with extremely complicated issues, must cause even the most confident investigator to doubt whether it is possible to make any appreciable progress toward psychiatric knowledge and understanding; indeed, it has not been very long since some of our best researchers turned to related disciplines in search of rewards not afforded by psychotherapy. But psychiatry can look back with pride on the ground already covered and be assured that nothing in the future will impede its progress. Within the span of one century we have made advances comparable in every respect to those scored in other fields of medical science.

One Hundred Years of Psychiatry

by EMIL KRAEPELIN

Philosophical Library

New York

This work has been selected by scholars as being culturally important, and is part of the knowledge base of civilization as we know it. This work was reproduced from the original artifact, and remains as true to the original work as possible. Therefore, you will see the original copyright references, library stamps (as most of these works have been housed in our most important libraries around the world), and other notations in the work.

This work is in the public domain in the United States of America, and possibly other nations. Within the United States, you may freely copy and distribute this work, as no entity (individual or corporate) has a copyright on the body of the work.

As a reproduction of a historical artifact, this work may contain missing or blurred pages, poor pictures, errant marks, etc. Scholars believe, and we concur, that this work is important enough to be preserved, reproduced, and made generally available to the public. We appreciate your support of the preservation process, and thank you for being an important part of keeping this knowledge alive and relevant.

One Hundred Years Of Psychiatry

Emil Kraepelin

MAY 1963

ONE HUNDRED YEARS OF PSYCHIATRY

132 K91o   63-09784
Kraepelin
One hundred years of Psychiatry

During the eighteenth century the plight of the mentally ill was shocking almost everywhere in Europe. We know that they were generally handled like idlers, vagrants and criminals; the punitive laws to which they were subjected were rarely administered humanely. Some were allowed through the benevolence of their fellow men to eke out a penurious existence as beggars or harmless lunatics. Flighty, troublesome or dangerous patients were restrained and kept in a small room or stall in a private house, in "lunatic boxes," in cages or in other places of confinement that seemed appropriate for isolating them and rendering them harmless. Only a few of them were admitted to hospitals, such as the Juliusspital in Würzburg, where they could receive special attention and medical care. As a result of poor supervision, many committed suicide, perished through accidents or created serious disturbances. The tense and exasperating environment thus created encouraged the establishment of the strictest preventive measures.

There were in Germany at that time no special institutions for the insane but only wards in poorhouses, prisons, orphanages, workhouses and hospitals in which troublesome mental patients were confined. "We lock these unfortunate creatures in lunatic cells, as if they were criminals," exclaimed Reil in 1803, "We keep them in chains in forlorn jails, near the roosts of owls in hidden recesses above the gates of towns, or in the damp cellars of reformatories where no sympathetic human being can ever bestow on them a friendly glance, and we let them rot in their own filth. Their fetters scrape the flesh from their bones, and their wan, hollow faces search for the grave that their wailing and our ignominy conceals from them." Writers of that time never tired of setting down terrifying descriptions of the insane and their surroundings. One anonymous reporter wrote in 1795: "A humanitarian is bound to shudder when he discovers the plight of the unfortunate victims of this dreadful affliction; many of them grovel in their own filth on unclean straw that is seldom changed, often stark naked and in chains, in dark, damp dungeons where no breath of fresh air can enter. Under such terrifying conditions, it would be easier for the most rational person to become insane than for a madman to regain his sanity." He added that in one so-called asylum which he visited, five out of nine died during the summer. In 1818 Esquirol in Paris wrote in the same vein to the minister of the interior: "I saw patients naked, with rags or nothing more than straw to protect them against the cold, damp weather. I saw how in their wretched state they were deprived of fresh air to breathe, of water to quench their thirst, and of the basic necessities of life. I saw them turned over for safekeeping to brutal jailors. I saw them chained in damp, cramped holes without light or air; people would be ashamed to keep in such places the wild animals which are cared for at great expense in our large cities. That is what I observed almost everywhere in France, and that is how the mentally ill are treated almost everywhere in Europe."

"It is indeed frightening," explained Frank in 1804, "to approach such a wretched and sorrowful place! To hear mingled shouts of exultation and despair and then to think that within are human beings once renowned for their talent and sensitivity. It is terrifying to go inside and be assailed by these filthy, ragged creatures, while others are prevented from joining in the assault only by their fetters and chains or by the jabs of their attendants." In the same year Hoch reported: "In the asylum in Berlin

11

those who are stark raving mad are isolated for the duration of their madness; they are locked naked in small cages or hutches, and food and water are introduced through holes and placed in copper basins secured by chains." He recommended that asylums be established in remote, isolated places since the wailing and howling of deranged patients disturbed all sane men and upset the whole community. Stupid or mentally deficient patients, because they seemed passively to endure whatever was inflicted upon them, gave rise to the popular assumption (rejected by Tuke) that they were insensitive to hunger, cold, and pain even though the opposite was proven by their obvious emaciation, by their frozen members, and by their dying from injuries. The result was that their suffering was looked upon as self-evident and unalterable while the significance of their plight was never fully appreciated.

The conditions just described persisted until well along in the nineteenth century. In 1842 an investigation of housing conditions in Holland revealed patients "lying naked on filthy straw in foul air, frequently in chains, under a blanket; many were without sufficient food; men and women were indiscriminately mingled, and to all appearances some of them had not seen daylight for a long time." But in 1843 Mahir described the present-day Narrenturm in Vienna (a circular five-story building with room in its 139 cells for between 200 and 250 mental patients) in these words: "The dark cells and corridors, secured by massive iron doors and gates and by awesome chains and locks, strongly suggest its prison-like character; to escape from it would defy the efforts of the most accomplished criminal or miscreant. The doctors who visit this dungeon are greeted by its inordinate filth, by its abominable, unbearable stench, noise and howling, and by the terrifying, heart-rending cries of many lunatics whose arms and legs—or even necks—are cruelly shackled in heavy chains and iron rings. I have seen many wretched mental patients, but the most wretched of all were those who had been caged and treated like wild beasts. Not even the worst menagerie would exhibit such unfriendly, inhumane conditions. The faces and actions of the lunatics revealed their intense pain, suffering and despair. Their meager fare and their unending physical suffering, aggravated by the senseless application of vesicants and pustulants, made their plight worse than that of even the most vicious criminals and murderers, for these piteous creatures never saw a ray of sunshine nor the full light of day. A tiny hole guarded by a heavy iron grill was the only opening through which diagnosis and treatment could be accomplished. The attending physician was greeted by weeping and wailing, by insults and imprecations. Through the same hole brutal, unsympathetic wardens pushed food and drink for the much abused madmen, as if they were wolves and hyenas."

—Chains were commonly used a hundred years ago to shackle patients to the wall or to rings in the floor. Physicians then entertained an unwarranted fear of lunatics, as laymen still do, and ascribed to them extraordinary physical strength because of their rash conduct. No effort was spared to render them harmless. On his official visit to Juliusspital in 1700 Müller found in the middle of each ward for mental patients a huge stone post with chains suitable for subduing and "disciplining restless or troublesome patients." Hayner also noted that in Waldheim it was not until 1807 that he managed to abolish

13

"the abominable use" of chains. Conolly alleged that in a large private institution in England 70 out of 400 patients were kept in chains almost continuously for a period of twenty years.

Those who visited Bedlam in London in 1814 could see countless patients clad only in loose shrouds and chained by their arms or legs to the wall in such a way that they could stand upright or remain seated. One patient for twelve years wore rings around his neck and waist and was tethered to a wall; because he had resisted attempts to control his movements by means of a chain manipulated from a neighboring room, the warden had also taken the precaution of lashing his arms to his sides. An administrator explained that chains were the surest device for restraining recalcitrant mental patients. Even Dr. Monro stated in response to an investigating committee of the House of Commons that no one dared use chains on noblemen, but that they were indispensable in dealing with the poor and with those in public institutions. Gùntz in his travels noted that in 1853 in Gheel (Belgium) fetters and chains were still in use.

Rivaling chains in popularity was the lash. Müller related that in the Juliusspital attendants were generously provided with many restraining and punitive devices—chains, manacles, shackles, and efficient, leather-encased bullwhips. They made ample use of these instruments whenever a patient complained, littered his quarters, or became recalcitrant or abusive. "Thrashing was almost a part of the daily routine," he concluded. Lichtenberg explained that thrashings were often better for lunatics than anything else, and that they helped them to adjust to the harsh realities of daily life. Even Reil, the enthusiastic champion of mental care for the insane, noted that the strait jacket, confinement, hunger, and a few lashes with the bullwhip would readily bring patients into line.

Frank was also of the opinion that "a light blow" was "effective in dealing with malicious or unreasonable patients." Autenrieth found that women who persisted in going around naked quickly dressed in response to a few applications of the lash. Neumann recommended the lash for uncleanliness. He said that it was generally effective, especially when benevolently applied. Langermann, the highly esteemed reformer who worked with Prussian mental patients, wrote as late as 1804 that doctors should when necessary resort to imprisonment, punishment, and flogging. Hayner in 1817 spoke out vehemently against physical chastisement of the insane, calling it unjustified, shameful, and unnecessary. "From this day on," he exclaimed, "let no one strike a single victim from the piteous ranks of these patients! I curse any man, great or small, who sanctions the beating of a man devoid of understanding!"

Not until much later, however, did corporal punishment disappear completely from institutions for the insane. Horn stated in 1818 that there could be no comparison between cases helped by punishment and those harmed by it, and he objected to the practice "in some institutions for the insane" of repaying in kind a patient who struck a doctor or an attendant. But Amelung was still maintaining in 1834 that punishment was mandatory "especially in dealing with stubborn, recalcitrant, or at times even wilfully filthy and malicious patients who possess some measure of sound judgment." As late as 1845, the superintendent of the Stralsund asserted that a few lashes with the birch rod could do wonders for persistent uncleanliness. He had in mind not only the inflicting of pain but

15

also the vigorous stimulation of the glutei, which "obviously exerted a favorable influence on the sphincter muscles of the bladder and consequently of the anus."

Perfected and modified according to circumstances, chains gave way to a long series of other ingenious contrivances, all designed to limit the patient's freedom of movement. According to Oegg, restraining devices were generally thought to be as necessary for the preservation of life as eating, drinking, etc. First place went to the strait jacket or camisole, devised by MacBride and highly recommended by Cullen. Long blind sleeves made it possible to secure the patient's arms against his chest or back. According to Willis (1822) the strait jacket soothed the mind, induced reflection, prevented overexcitement, encouraged relaxation, and also had the desirable effect of increasing perspiration. According to Haslam, however, when too tight, it interfered with respiration and the circulation of the blood and prevented the patient from wiping his nose, scratching, or driving away flies. His objections were refuted by Vering, who found that the benefits derived from wearing the strait jacket increased with the patient's discomfort. Neumann recommended it for quarrelsome and bellicose women "because restraining them made them "look repulsive."

Another device was the leather girdle provided with straps or mufflike gloves for immobilizing the lunatic's hands. In some instances leather gloves joined at the wrists were sufficient to prevent patients from scratching, mutilating themselves, or masturbating. Once he had been subdued and lashed to the wall with the help of the strait jacket, a patient inclined to run away or to kick the attendant had his feet bound or placed inside a cylinder made of wicker or tin.

Extensive use was made of the "tranquilizer" introduced by Rush. This restraining chair was equipped with supports to which the body, legs, and arms could be lashed. In a few hours, according to Willis, it would make the most stubborn and irascible patient gentle and submissive. Horn remarked that it had a remarkable effect on the psychology of the patient. "He must tolerate having his body in an uncomfortable or a painful position... The new and unpleasant situation engages his attention and directs it toward something external. Sooner or later he regains his self-esteem. He often emerges calm, thoughtful and tractable." Groos treasured the restraining chair to such an extent that he repeatedly stated, according to Roller, that without it he would not care to be an alienist. Heinroth publicly recommended it as the best restraining device known to him for transforming many unruly individuals in dark, isolated places into gentle, submissive men and women. Jacobi took issue with him and cited a patient who had spent six consecutive months in the restraining chair. Blumroder also maintained that restraint aggravated the lunatic's condition, prolonging and intensifying his resistance. "The sanest man would soon agree with me," he added, "if he spent half an hour on a restraining chair, unable to scratch a fleabite."

Similar in purpose to the "tranquilizer" was the restraining bed, which could immobilize a patient in a strait jacket. It was provided with a slit for the disposal of refuse, or sometimes with straw-covered wire netting.

Patients were entrusted to the care of attendants generally described as uncouth, unsympathetic, rude and untidy. "Male attendants were usually selected because of their physical strength and defiant appearance," wrote Müller. "At heart they might be the opposite. The main qualities sought in female attendants were likewise strong muscles and bones, courage, and a sharp tongue." The result was that the worst misfits were selected as attendants. Horn stated that the rabble of Berlin could not be worse than the attendants in its hospital; that the individuals who applied for positions must have been the worst in the city "for they inspire or merit such little trust that the average person would hesitate to employ them as household servants." It was even decided for reasons of economy to employ ex-convicts, and this policy was followed for years in the new Sonnenstein sanatorium. As late as 1846 Mahir recommended the employment of disabled veterans for reasons of economy.

Such conditions are not surprising, for according to a rumor which originated in France in 1785, most people who cared for the mentally ill eventually became delirious or insane. Esquirol frankly observed that, though during forty years he had seen nothing to corroborate it, the belief was prevalent in most countries, especially in Germany. That there was a general scarcity of attendants is easily understandable, however, since working in a ward for the insane then held no appeal. An attendant had to care for from thirty to fifty patients. This entailed giving him the right to restrain or punish patients at will.

We can easily imagine what such hospitals looked like and what went on inside them. A painting by Hogarth reveals many interesting details. The isolated rooms in which most patients spent their days were without air or light; heavily barred windows and massive bolted doors, solid except for small peepholes, gave them a dungeonlike appearance. Gutters in the stone floors of cells were designed to carry off the refuse, with the result that pungent odors filled the air. A cell generally contained a hutch-like bed, made of either wood or stone; fastened to the wall and covered with straw, it was often provided with a sewer. Sometimes it contained a restraining chair and a corner toilet that could be emptied from outside the cell. In their cramped, dirty, friendless quarters patients had nothing except what was riveted or nailed to the walls or floor. Windows were covered with latticework, stoves were provided with strong fire-guards, and benches and tables were securely held in place. Table utensils were made of tin or wood. Clothing was made of a single strip of ticking or coarse canvas, often trimmed with leather. Strips of leather were also used to trim belts and to secure gloves, strait jackets, and masks. Some patients were locked in cages. The barren yard was surrounded by insurmountable walls.

Lazy, indifferent, incompetent attendants were unable to cope with the problem of feeding the helpless or maintaining cleanliness in quarters teeming with dribbling, vomiting, defecating patients. Conolly reported that in an institution for 176 patients a single towel was deemed satisfactory. It is not surprising that every insane ward was permeated by a peculiar smell described by van Swieten and Boerhave and singled out by Friedrich in 1836 as a sure symptom of insanity. Vermin also thrived In many institutions there were countless rats; Esquirol said that these rats sometimes gnawed on paralytic or imbecile patients. To all this the teeming patients added their shouting and wailing, their bickering and quarreling; their ceaseless attempts to break their bonds, to destroy everything within reach, to inflict harm upon themselves or others; all the eccentric and terrifying patterns of behavior that have created the popular image of the "Snake Pit." "The nocturnal raving of the insane and the clanking of their chains," wrote Reil, "echo day and night through the long corridors lined with their cages, and soon destroy what little sanity the newcomer still retains."

Until the beginning of the nineteenth century asylums were open to the curious for their amusement. In 1799 Kant warned nervous people against visiting institutions for the insane out of curiosity because the sight of the patients might through the intermediacy of the imagination provoke similar disturbances in the onlookers. "Avoid this," he added, "if you care about your sanity." Pinel observed that anyone with an admission ticket was allowed to enter the insane ward in the Salpêtrière. Müller also noted that in the Juliusspital the worst paid attendants and porters earned money illegally by allowing visitors to tease, excite and stare at unfortunate lunatics as if they were animals in a menagerie; moreover, this situation often created a distorted picture of their derangement. He related that he himself, unable to dissuade a count, his bride, and his father-in-law from wanting to see the lunatics, took them to a nymphomaniac who "in her negligee" put her arms around the father-in-law's neck and smothered him with kisses. "I believe," he concluded "that it will be a long time before he again wants to see lunatics." In 1844 Ramaer reported that in Zütphen until the beginning of the past year curiosity seekers had been able on payment of a small gratuity to observe the insane.

Still the picture of the old insane asylum is incomplete. The pressure of restraining devices, which had to be firmly applied to accomplish their purpose, frequently caused swelling, ulcers, and even paralysis and gangrene in the affected members. Filth and immobility aggravated the gangrenous condition. Food was generally scarce and unvaried. Hunger pangs were the rule since, as Langermann pointed out in 1804, the common notion was that mental patients required a meager and restricted diet. At night patients were generally left to themselves. Lacking proper supervision, they often fought bitterly, engaging in what Müller called bullfights and meting out to each other severe injuries. Fettered patients often succeeded in gaining their freedom by force or with the assistance of fellow sufferers, then committed suicide or made vicious attacks on their surroundings. The incidence of disease, injuries and accidents was alarming. Pinel reported that 57 out of 110 patients died in 1784 and 95 out of 151 in 1788; and even later death claimed between one-third and one-fourth of all mental patients. Conolly put the mortality rate in English institutions over a twenty-year period at 14% or higher. The frequent "disappearance" of patients prompted a searching investigation of conditions prevalent in private English asylums in 1815. The investigators uncovered some startling details. They found, for example, that efforts to conceal the facts had resulted in falsification of vital statistics and that patients who had "disappeared" were entered on the records as "discharged." After an investigation into conditions in the old York County asylum was initiated in 1813, a fire destroyed the main part of the building along with most of the records and documents. The superintendent had full knowledge of the fire in which many patients perished. "Just how many perished," added Conolly, "was never ascertained."

The widespread abuses described here owed their origin to two false suppositions adopted by the public at large as well as by many physicians. The first was the notion that mental illnesses were incurable. Larochefoucault-Lianfourt in his report to the constitutional assembly on conditions

Emil Kraepelin

in the insane asylums in France stated: "Insanity is regarded as incurable. The insane receive no medical treatment. Those considered dangerous are chained like wild beasts." "One of mankind's most deplorable prejudices concerns insanity," said Pinel. "Probably because the insane are almost universally neglected, their illness is considered incurable." And Davis explained: "The unfortunate lunatic is given his dole of bread and water. Incapable of providing for himself, he is allowed to lie on his straw-covered bed chained to the wall in his dark, lonely cell, a victim of the convenient and selfish notion that insanity is an incurable illness." According to Damerow, the notion was not refuted until the second decade of the nineteenth century when a distinction was first made between custodial hospital care and active treatment centers. Only then was it found that great numbers of mental patients could be rehabilitated. Griesinger also inferred that the possibility of rehabilitating a certain proportion of the mentally ill was first discovered around 1820. That a few patients under constant care had previously recovered, even under unfavorable conditions, was obviously proven by records of the Juliusspital. But these isolated cases were obliterated by the staggering fact that the overwhelming majority of patients confined to asylums either perished or reverted to the most shocking patterns of bestiality. The results are explained by the tendency to turn to such institutions for help only in cases of protracted illness, long after all hope had been abandoned. We can be sure, however, that many patients who might have recovered under proper treatment succumbed as a result of their confinement in the asylum. Mental patients created an atmosphere of intense, terrifying suffering, and there was little to suggest that their plight could ever be alleviated. It is no wonder, therefore, that people were intent upon finding the least painful way to render harmless loved ones in a hopeless condition.

To the notion that insanity was incurable was added the false supposition that the behavior of mental patients was an outward manifestation of innate weakness or baseness. Their behavior, whether ridiculous and degenerate or dangerous and terrifying, could not fail to draw attention to their plight and to cast a shadow over their relations. This accounts for the perpetuation of the notion that mental illness is not so much a misfortune as a disgrace for the patient and his family. The whole system of treatment was also predicated on the assumption that mental patients are habitually disordered, malicious, base creatures. Every attempt was made to force them to renounce their foolishness and to bring them to submission by abusing and punishing them. When abuse and punishment failed, they had to be rendered harmless. Their freedom of movement was restricted to the utmost, and they were watched over like wild beasts.

Their eccentric and unpredictable behavior caused patients to appear more rational in many ways than they actually were and to be held in awe. The result was that the improper treatment to which they were then subjected merely reinforced their hostility. Inevitably they developed an abiding resentment toward their tormentors, and this culminated in a relentless and ruthless struggle against all forms of oppression. That is why patients in the old asylums were depicted as raving, raging hords of degenerate creatures likely at any moment to give vent to their fury through savage attacks or acts of violence unless held in check by brute force. Esquirol reported that in many French institutions attendants relied on dogs for protection. Reil proposed that attendants wear invisible coats of mail when performing their duties inside the lunatics' cells. For apprehending patients who had to be put in fetters, German attendants used semicircular "catching-sticks" to pin them against the wall before overpowering them.

Stemming from and complicating these attitudes relating to the plight of mental patients was the scarcity of alienists. A century ago the treatment of the insane was entrusted almost exclusively to the supervisor, superintendent or director of the institution. Physicians were consulted only in case of physical ailments. Among contemporary writers who dealt with the subject of insanity we find such noted laymen, theologians and philosophers as Beneke, Hoffbauer, Fries and Kant. Haslam was a pharmacist. Such men as Reil and Autenrieth, and indeed even Nasse and Friedrich, had little or no psychiatric training even though they were physicians. A few outstanding men advanced the science of psychiatry by devoting their lives to the study and treatment of mental patiens: Lorry, Daquin, Pinel and Esquirol in France; Cullen, Arnold, Perfect, Pargeter and Crichton in England; Chiarugi in Italy; Reil, Heinroth, Horn, Hayner and Pienitz in Germany. In addition, in scattered hospitals and asylums there were a few doctors who had acquired some knowledge of insanity by long and patient observation of mental patients. They had little professional training, however, and treated the insane only incidentally. They can hardly be said to have been mainly interested in the science of psychiatry. Besides, they held inferior positions in the institutions and could have little influence on the plight of the patients. Even Müller reported that in Wurzburg he had to submit formal written requests to be allowed to see patients desperately in need of his services, that refusals were transmitted to him orally by the porter, that he had no voice in hiring or firing attendants, and that it was not until 1816 that doctors were addressed as *Herr*. Similar complaints came from other sources. Then as now psychiatric treatment was held in low repute. In England it was assumed that two visits a week by a qualified general practitioner from the vicinity were sufficient for private institutions with fewer than one hundred patients. In 1821 Nasse, the revered German proponent of scientific psychiatry, was still maintaining that the care of harmless lunatics should be entrusted to the clergy.  Even after psychiatric treatment gained favor, the number of trained physicians was too small and their remuneration wholly inadequate. These circumstances explain the failure of the new science to develop rapidly.

Professor Autenrieth in Tübingen in his lectures on mental ailments warned his students that they risked losing their own sanity or becoming lunatics if they spent too much time in treating mental patients. While we scarcely dare take for granted that training in psychiatry is on a significantly higher plane today, we know that psychiatric clinics in the modern sense did not exist for a long time. Clinical lectures on psychiatry were held in various places, but as late as 1838 Roller could still state: "A clinic for the insane is something designed to solve an unsolved and insoluble problem." Characteristic of the notions prevalent on this issue one hundred years ago were the plans developed in 1819 by Nasse, an ardent proponent of psychiatric instruction for physicians, for the construction of clinical wards for mental patients. In them he provided space for six or eight patients who might be replaced every two or three months by lunatics from a neighboring asylum. He recommended that of three professors—an internalist, a surgeon, and an obstretrician—the one best qualified should at first take it upon himself to offer instruction in psychiatry, and that later the internalist should be required to possess the necessary qualifications for the assignment. It is worth noting that considerable controversy still revolves around the practice of delivering a clinical lecture in the presence of patients.

It is obvious that the science of psychiatry was still in its infancy a century ago. What we find most striking about the work of psychiatrists is the stress on observation and interpretation of data In their discussions and meditations they emphasized the scientific method. "People reason too much and observe too little," wrote Reil in 1803. As late as 1822, Jacobi complained that the total available number of pertinent studies was much too insignificant to serve as a valid basis for a uniform system. Because of the slipperiness of the terrain, the difficulty of close observation, and the danger of falling victim to deception and reaching false conclusions, he emphasized the necessity of adhering strictly to a policy of methodical investigation and prudent induction.

At the end of the eighteenth century the alienist used as his starting point philosophy or anthropology, which Kant defined as practical psychology. Thus Daquin wrote in 1792 "The Philosophy of Madness—A Philosophical Essay on Persons Afflicted by Madness," and Pinel published (1800) his "Medicophilosophical Treatise on Mental Alienation or Madness" in which he cited a patient whose symptoms could be described "in terms used by Locke and Condillac in connection with insanity." Ruhland in 1801 published his "Medicophilosophical Treatises on the Concept of Mental Disorders," and Ideler explained that psychiatry was the bridge between medicine and philosophy. In his work on anthropology Kant gave a detailed account of his views of insanity in its diverse forms, but he also denied outright that legal pharmacy or even legal medicine could establish whether a criminal was sane or insane at the time his crime was committed. He held that such cases were within the sphere of philosophy. Nor did he hesitate, though he lacked experience in medicine, to formulate a theory of mental illnesses and their probable patterns of development.

We find in textbooks and in leading medical journals lengthy discussions of the relation between body and mind, of the belief of immortality, of the unity of separation between body and soul, etc. Researchers tended to interpret findings naively and arbitrarily, or to discover general relationships between the most disparate sets of conditions. From the correspondence between our concept of the soul and the shape of the brain, for example, Burdach deduced that the brain was the organ of the soul. Grohmann connected the activity of the brain with the individual's philosophy of life, in which the number three played a dominant role. He reasoned that just as the natural kingdoms stretched from earth to sky to the source of light, so the structures within our bodies included the abdomen, the breast, and the brain, which in turn consisted of the spinal column, the cerebellum, and the cerebrum; and that sensory progression from smell to hearing to sight was matched by the inorganic forces of vegetation, expansion, and contraction and by the organic forces of production, irritability, and sensibility.

Following a similar course of reasoning Damerow in 1829 developed the theory that the three body cavities corresponded to three different temperaments: the head and brains to the choleric, the breast and spinal column to the sanguine, and the ganglia and bowels to the melancholic. After equating the senses, the nerves and the reproductive system with the three divisions of the brain—the two hemispheres and the cerebellum—he expanded the correspondence to sensibility, movement, and nutrition, and likened animal consciousness, affect and instinct to human understanding, imagination and will. This tripartition extended even to fish, ventral water animals containing the germ of melancholic or venous elements; to birds, pectoral air animals classed as sanguine; and to mammals, especially carnivores, "earth (fire) and cranial animals" with a choleric temperament. Finally, mineral prescriptions were supposed to affect the reproductive, the vegetable and the irritable system while animal prescriptions affected the sensory system.

Concepts developed by the chemists and by the discovery of galvanism, electricity, and magnetism, which was still confused with so-called animal magnetism, were related to psychic phenomena and mental illnesses. Thus Heinroth related the two main types of mental disturbances, delirium and melancholia, to two opposing physical forces: centripetal force or contraction, which causes a body moving around a center to move inward and be lost in nothingness; and centrifugal force or expansion, which causes a body to move outward and be lost in nothingness. "We find the physical equivalents of these two forces in oxygen and in hydrogen: the former in connection with metals and the latter with plants. Both bear a certain resemblance to poison, but they differ in that the metallic poison destroys from within while botanical narcosis affects the periphery." Using such arguments he attempted "by example and by analogy" to prove that melancholia and delirium were similar to contrasting physical forces.

Blumröder believed that insanity and epileptic seizures had a common origin and that excessive accumulations of electricity were discharged through convulsions that "robbed the nervous system and depleted its energy." To illuminate a murderer's temperament, Class compared the latter's oblong organs with his spherical ones and deduced a corresponding ration between centripetal and centrifugal forces as well as two opposing tendencies—timidity and rashness. He supposed that a thick brain with uniform hardening from the back to the front indicated a weak mind with a good memory; that the "power of attraction" corresponded to the positive pole, to oxygen, to excessive coagulation and rigidity, and to all phenomena relating to acidification; and that the "power of repulsion" corresponded to the negative pole, to round organs, to combustion, and to suppleness since it was responsible for hydrogenation. Damerow felt certain that scirrhous tumors, cancerous hardenings of the breast, stomach and uterus, lithiasis and the like could result from changes in temperament. He regarded these morbid products as "a type of chemical-organic precipitation" of psychic suffering organically discharged in such a way as to externalize an inner pain and give it rigid permanence, perhaps on account of the intimate correlation of psychic suffering with the depositing of tangible, concentrated materials: "They may well be organic reflexes or pathological forms or symbols of psychic suffering."

The last and most extravagant course of reasoning involving natural philosophy is found in Kieser's book *Elements of Psychiatry* (1855). In the first part of the

Philippe Pinel

book one can read whole pages and still not understand a single sentence. Kieser's student Feuerstein explained mental diseases through a reversal or displacement of polarity. He posited as their immediate cause an abnormal, involuntary oscillation in a peripheral portion of the brain. Walther went so far as to posit the quadruplicity of the regions of the world as the objectification of the quadruplicity of the mind. He related mind and the north to carbon, reason and the west to hydrogen, imagination and the south to nitrogen, and understanding and the east to oxygen. These and other eccentric musings were complemented by magazine articles on telepathy and clairvoyance, on fortunetelling and divination, on animal magnetism, and even on dowsing rods.

During the early years of the last century German scientific publications gave scant attention to case histories, which were generally used not as points of departure for valid conclusions but rather as embellishments for unverified generalizations; both their brevity and their emphasis on singularity gave them an anecdotal character. A few extraordinary tales, some of them even drawn from antiquity or from poets, were cited repeatedly, with nothing to substantiate their credibility, as documentary evidence. We also find in scientific publications inexplicable conclusions purportedly based on observation. Neumann, for example, concluded that the patient's cranium shrank and that the back part became appreciably flatter and lower as the patient became more and more demented.

Most writers of the period who dealt with psychiatry lacked the practical experience that would qualify them for the undertaking. Kant and Hegel tried to explain mental illnesses on the basis of common knowledge.

Even the doctors who worked in mental wards had scant opportunity to carry out exhaustive research, for both the size of the wards and the number of yearly admissions were too small. From 1798 to 1823 Juliusspital, which had one of the oldest and best wards in Europe, admitted on the average 21 patients a year, though it could accommodate seventy. Admissions to Pinel's ward in Paris rarely averaged more than 170 or 190. That a science constantly influenced by natural phenomena could evolve but slowly under these conditions is readily understandable. While French alienists worked under more favorable conditions and accumulated a vast store of data based on direct observation, the most famous and most stimulating work produced by the old school of German psychiatry, Reil's rhapsodies on the application of the psychic method of treatment of mental disorders, characteristically came from the pen of a man who eight years later still had little or no experience in psychiatry and whose incompetence was clearly reflected in his writing. Autenrieth wrote a treatise on psychiatry after he had had the opportunity to observe 28 patients during a ten-year period.

Contemporary views relating to the nature and cause of insanity also reflected the orientation of medical thought, with its emphasis on imagination rather than on methodical observation. A focal point of discussion was the question of whether mental disturbances have their origin in psychic changes or in somatic changes. Proponents of the psychic theory, led by Professor Heinroth of Leipzig, who defended the unity of body and mind, regarded insanity as the effluence of personal guilt, which is "the source of all evil as well as of all psychic disturbances." In the struggle between human selfishness and lofty ideals

33

dictated by reason, the voice of our conscience provides a compass which we can use for our guidance or disregard. The man who seeks worldly pleasures and the satisfaction of his ego is committing a sin and thwarting the realization of his full potentialities—in short, he is impairing his development as a rational, well-organized being. His transgression against the higher life checks, limits, and impairs his own existence as a human being.... By giving himself over to evil man becomes a slave to ungodliness and eventually loses not only his sense of discretion but also his freedom and his concern for wholesome pleasures and true happiness. A prey to suffering, illusion, and oppression, he finds his creative capacity severely restricted, thwarted, and forced to assume a secondary role. Thus by studying the effect of disturbances in the internal organization of an individual on his free development, we have evolved the concept of psychic illness. Since the psyche is independently free, it can lose its freedom only by attaching itself to sin. It thrives when independent and sickens in the presence of guilt, sin, or selfishness. The same applies to the origin of psychic disturbances; the mother is pure psyche; the procreator is evil which, using a many-sided approach, mates with the psyche. "The psyche and evil are united just as the sexes are universally united: through love. The psyche's love for evil is called its propensity for evil." So he explains the psyche's faltering, downfall, and plunge into the abyss of darkness. "Men may say what they will, but apart from total denial of God there is no psychic disorder. It follows that an evil spirit dwells in those who suffer from psychic disorders; they are truly possessed."

Heinroth repeatedly emphasized that he found proof

everywhere that psychic disorders had their origin in the voluntary pursuit of evil. He held that *melancholia attonita* resulted from an experience that made a profound impression on a mind incapable of offering effective resistance "since the individual had failed during his lifetime to make the necessary preparation"; that indecision and exhaustion *(abulia melancholia)* developed as a result of exhaustion but not (like *abulia simplex*) in the absence of prior guilt; and that indecision coupled with madness *(abulia anoa)* was "the result of sexual promiscuity." He assumed that "melancholia accompanying mental derangement, delirium, and insanity" developed "partly from dissolute and extravagant living, partly from a sinful and criminal pattern of behavior in an excessively energetic individual," while "madness" and *mania simplex* were characteristic of a sinful will and had their origins in man's degenerate moral anlage. Madness in general *(eknoia catholica)* was attributed by Heinroth to "intense suffering, rash and misguided thinking, and impulsive behavior." About frantic behavior *(eknoia maniaca)* he wrote: "From this hell there is no salvation other than through a miracle. Only through the most hideous forms of debasement, through the vilest excesses, and through the worst crimes can a man in this condition achieve complete psychic catharsis." Finally, he assumed that religious melancholia resulted from worldliness, from foolish conduct, from falling into a dissolute life, and ultimately from the man's troubled conscience, which terrified his defenseless mind. "A dissolute life that has sapped his strength, wanton surrender to every passion, a serious crime or a series of offenses—this is the boggy pond whose dregs foam to the surface following a violent disturbance of its depths. A shattered psyche in a shattered body—this is the basis for religious melancholia." One should not be deceived by the appearance of innocence, he warned, since this might be mere whitewash. The actions of lunatics, viewed in the wrong light and grossly misinterpreted on account of these false hypotheses, were labeled monstrous and shocking.

Heinroth obviously had to resort to facile arguments to support his theory. Only a dissolute life in which the search for what is highest and noblest has no part, he argued, could constitute a diathesis to numerous mental disorders that vary according to temperament. Influenced by the total pattern of living elaborated in accordance with his inner nature and his own free will, the individual acquires a disposition to be either creative or destructive. When external influences like shock, anger and grief bring about mental disorders, "this is proof positive that such individuals are anything but mentally sound, that they are indeed morally corrupt." Methodical analysis of the facts would show that "only by positing a positive susceptibility to sickness *brought about by* misguided life could these stimuli have produced such striking results." Excessive eating, indigestion, tainted or highly seasoned foods, exposure to heat or cold, the whole gamut of rash actions that impair health and entail sundry consequences that endanger body and soul—can all this "be the sign of a well-ordered psychic life? Or it is not rather an indication that the organization of the psyche is defective? Gross negligence, thoughtlessness, rashness, violence—in short, all types of aberrant behavior associated with mental disorders—can hardly be accounted for if we assume that its organization is perfect." Concerning the alleged morbific influence of repressed hemorrhoids, he wrote: "Do they result from a wholesome pattern of living?

From a good physical and mental regimen? Age, constitution, etc. may play a part, but no such disorders occur in the absence of dissipation, laxity, imprudence, etc. Gluttony, intemperance, dissolute living—all this finally forces nature to resort to extreme measures in an attempt to effect a cure. This hardly redounds to the credit of mankind!"

Heinroth extolled the efficacy of blood-letting in the treatment of mania. Though he advocated letting the hot blood gush from the veins "as if rejoicing over its escape from the prison in which it was raging," he denied any connection between his treatment and the origin of the affliction. He thought rather in terms of a diseased state of the vascular system and its contents, which he looked upon as the end result and sure stamp of a radically disorganized life—a life robbed of a sense of proportion and organization by unnatural psychic and somatic deportment, by emotional excesses, by intemperance, and especially by sensuality.

From such notions Heinroth naturally drew the conclusion that the only defense against insanity was faith, and he devoted the ethical or prophylactic section of his book to proving his point. "Faith penetrates to the very roots of our earthly existence, fortifying and strengthening us. As long as it permeates our bodies it affords protection against all mental disorders and temptations. It is the one sure defense identified by our search." Thus he proved that whoever took the necessary precautions would never lose his sanity or become mentally ill. In 1838 Groos concluded, after investigating the question of whether a level-headed man could become insane, that the mind could be adversely affected by a sudden blow on the forehead or by a dose of belladonna while a normal person would not evidence the frightful bewilderment, baffling absurdities, unnatural passions and depraved longings characteristic of lunacy but would fall into a trance or light coma which would entail none of these loathsome symptoms.

Similar to Heinroth's views were those of Ideler, who detected in uncontrolled passions the mainspring of mental disorders and even of physical ailments. He called attention to the fact that "as every experienced doctor knows, almost all mental disorders with the exception of those resulting from poisoning or injuries (if we broaden the latter term to make it include contagion and miasmas) owe their origin directly to an emotional shock or develop from other causes under its influence."

The next step was to posit specific causes for specific disorders. Heinroth held that delirium, a dreamlike state of confusion, was always caused by violent emotions, namely love and jealousy; that melancholia resulted from grief, resentment and worry; and that different forms of mental derangement associated with delirium were brought about by pride, greed, ambition, avarice, conceit, arrogance, and fanaticism. Imbecility was attributed to debauchery, onanism, alcoholism and gluttony. Rage or frenzy was associated with wanton lawlessness which turned the individual against himself and his destiny and made him hostile toward laws and regulations, his enemies thereafter just as he had once been theirs. Frenzy was clearly the outward expression of the inner condition of the organism. "Aware of his separation from the good and despairing of the possibility of his ever again being united with it, he surrenders himself to destruction and corruption." We are reminded here of the words with which Burrows in 1828 began his book on mental disorders: "Insanity is the scourge brought down on sinful men by the wrath of the Almighty."

The most telling objections that could be raised against the views under discussion were soon brought to light. Animated discussions ensued. Heinroth tried by the line of reasoning previously outlined to invalidate the ready objection that not every mental patient had led a sinful life. He argued that every man was tainted by sin and that moral defects were revealed by vicious and by selfishness. Still other objections were based on the fact that insanity was frequently accompanied by physical changes that seemed to imply a casual relationship while psychic disorders could be caused by poisons, febrific illnesses, or damage to the brain. Countering objections based on a causal relationship was the argument that observed changes were not so much the cause as the result of psychic disorders. If a highly emotional person entertains and cherishes a notion or thought until it becomes a fixed idea, Heinroth explained, we should not be surprised but should rather expect to find that the delicate organs in the brain, cluttered with images of notions and ideas and adversely affected by overstimulation, overexcitement, etc., generate febrile or paralytic conditions. Organic troubles or disorders produced in this way can easily have a repercussion on the psyche, with the result that the subject, even if he has tired of his perverse life, can not return to normalcy but remains caught in the snare of his own devising. Or physical ailments produced by erratic behavior, debauchery, or immorality may also lay the foundation for the development of psychic disturbances.

Objections relating to the physical basis for psychic disorders were answered by eliminating from the sphere

Pinel at Salpêtrière

of insanity all mental disorders manifestly conditioned by physical suffering. Heinroth denied outright that somatic forces, physical injuries, mechanical or chemical agents, bodily illnesses, organic deficiencies, could be the idiopathic or primary cause of "true psychic disorders." He therefore made a distinction between true mental illnesses, characterized by the total absence of freedom, and "obstructed" conditions in which freedom is not completely destroyed but merely limited—or as he expressed it, momentarily obscured by a passing cloud. To him psychic disturbances produced by organic disorders were like clouds that hide the bright rays of the sun. He therefore made a rigid distinction between febrile delirium and ordinary types of insanity. Implicit in his reasoning, however, was the notion of mixed states, characterized by a blending of the two conditions—limited freedom and total absence of freedom. "Before succumbing to a febrile delirium," he reasoned, "none of these patients was virtuous enough to resist sinful impulses, temptations, passions, and especially immoral practices in his own life. Degenerate patterns of behavior may go undetected so long as the organic constitution is sound only to appear unexpectedly during an illness. The patient is like a drunkard whose intoxication brings to the surface his inner qualities."

As we would expect, such views were loudly protested by the "somatic" school of alienists. Laying greater emphasis on their medical training, they recalled the teachings of Hippocrates, who had clearly and categorically identified the brain as the seat of psychic processes and accordingly also as the source of psychic disorders. The coherence of the brain with both the organs of perception and the mechanism of locomotion, the close parallelism between psychic development and the structure of the brain in the animal kingdom and in the individual, and the obvious effect of disease and injury to the brain on the psyche supported the conviction that in the brain is to be sought, in Reil's words, "the matrix of our ego." This theory, defended by many alienists (e. g. Chiarugi and Willis), clashed sharply with moralistic and theological thinking. Its most outspoken champions, Nasse and Friedrich, emphatically contended that the immortal soul remained undamaged while the body became incapacitated through sickness and lacked the ability to give adequate expression to the prompting of the soul.

Jacobi occupied an exceptional position. Physical processes, no matter how they differ, can influence the psyche. Conversely, the activities of the psyche can affect every conceivable physical function. These two facts caused Jacobi to formulate the hypothesis that "organically conditioned psychic phenomena do not originate exclusively in the brain; the total organism is involved in their production, though the contribution of each of its parts may vary greatly both qualitatively and quantitatively." He reasoned that mental disorders were not to be considered independently but as expressions of various physical afflictions having their seat either in the brain or in some other part of the body—in the lungs, liver, intestines, heart, spleen, kidneys, blood vessels, or even in the skin, muscles or bones. "Any affliction or ailment, regardless of its symptoms and scope, regardless of the organs or regions affected by it, regardless of its nature—whether chronic or acute, intermittent or remittent, idiopathic or sympathetic—entails a characteristic modification of psychic phenomena." In this sense he was speaking not so much of mental illness as of "illness linked directly to insanity."

Jacobi also thought it likely that a madman, even if he could be equipped with a perfect brain, would still be unable to think logically; he held on the contrary that a lunatic, if he could be provided with a healthy body, might be more likely to benefit from the exchange since the vast reservoir of vegetative power inherent in the body might effect the reorganization of his diseased head. This view, while it necessarily underrated the causal significance of psychic endowment as well as emotional influences and gave undue weight to fortuitous physical disturbances, laid stress on the methodical study of mental patients and on post-mortem examinations. German researchers, often patterning their studies on investigations carried out by their French and English colleagues, provided scientific data for the elaboration of a clinical science of psychiatry.

Those who attempted to delineate the physiological bases of insanity were often on uncertain ground. Great importance was often attached to the neural fluid, humor, or ether purportedly identified in the brain; researchers assumed that this substance, when secreted in varying quantities, caused histological changes or engendered diverse disorders. Chiarugi laid particular stress on variations in the firmness of brain tissues and on the inordinate accumulation or depositing in the brain of morbific substances which "overpower, modify, and irritate" the brain. Many physicians stressed the pressure, movement, and composition of the blood that flowed through the brain and posited corresponding types of mental illnesses. Cox, who always sought the prime cause of insanity in the brain, looked first for a change in the circulation of the patient's blood, for a "cranial plethora." Even Rush thought that the prime cause of insanity lay in the blood vessels of the brain. Bird explained that a preponderance of arterial blood resulted in delirium while excessive venous blood produced melancholia. Marshal also came to the conclusion, mainly on the basis of post-mortem dissections, that mental disorders were as a rule closely related to cardiovascular irregularities affecting the brain. Crichton linked violent insanity to hypertension of the blood vessels, mild insanity to relaxation of tension, melancholia to complete blockage of circulation, and specific types of delirium to vascular disorders affecting particular organs. Arnold related the practice of bloodletting to a lessening of pressure on the cranial vessels and to their "unnatural activity."

Blumröder followed a similar course of reasoning. Making ample use of imagery, he related insanity to an interference in the relation between the calm reflective brain (phosphorus or *Ormuzd*) and the upsurge of blood symbolizing creative power *(Ahriman)*. In madness the brain was supposed to be dominated by the blood while in imbecility it was either "annihilated" by the upsurge of blood or rendered "impotent" by the total extinction of the "apparently electrical" energy of the brain. He held that other forms of mental derangement developed through an insufficiency or a superfluity of vitalizing blood at particular points in the brain, through changes in its condition, through the influence of contagious regions, or through the combining of arterial and venous blood. Blumröder said that cranial arteries carried "the most volatile, lightest, finest, most ethereal blood", and that this blood searched out the brain with "elective affinity," saturating and forcibly subduing it if its fibers were weak and inert but retreating if this brain could "think for itself."

Reil studied the general characteristics of tissues and concluded that dull, weak sensations associated with lunacy and imbecility developed when the nerves were too weak, the muscular fibers too tenuous, the gall insipid, and the reproductive organs inert, and that strong, lively sensations associated with madness or delirium were manifested when the albumen and fibrin were too thick and dry, the gall bitter, the fibers taut, and the reproductive organs highly responsive to stimuli. Still others elaborated the concept of irritation and its influence, directly or through the intermediacy of other organs, on the brain. Irritation was supposed to produce inflammation and bleeding and in this way to cause different types of mental disorders.

Antagonism between the different organs—between the vascular system and the nervous system, for example, and particularly between individual components of the nervous system—was given an important role in other attempts to explain insanity and prescribe treatment. Reil held that the two poles of the body—the head and the sex organs—acted and reacted on each other and that the same cause, an overcharge of electrical matter, might possibly create delirium in the head and lust in the sex organs. Agitation and excitement in one region could be linked to lethargy or paralysis in another. This explained on one hand the multiplicity of forms in which illnesses were manifested, and on the other the efficacy of measures applied in one region in correcting disorders in another. Guislain explained that as a rule the ultimate cause of mental disorders seemed to him to be a shift or displacement in the relation between the vascular system and the nervous system, between intelligence and emotion, freedom and restraint, mind and nature. The system of "indirect psychic treatment" described by Sandtmann, one of Horn's students, was based on similar considerations. His treatment was intended to influence the brain indirectly through antagonistic measures by arousing the emotions, inflicting pain, withholding basic necessities, cultivating disgust, or irritating the skin. An unnatural increase or diminution of activity in the central organ was supposed to be relayed to the organs lying beyond the center; the transfer made possible the reestablishment of the unity and perfect harmony of all organic activities. Jacobi, however, rejected such systems. He explained that methods of treatment elaborated on the basis of these concepts increased mortality while those who recovered were unable to find words to describe the horror of the mental states that they had experienced.

A century ago insanity was attributed to an imposing medley of morbific conditions. Naive but widespread was the foregone conclusion that any exceptional circumstance in the life of the patient was responsible for the onset of his affliction. A vast number of immediate causes was subsumed in Heinroth's theory that the ultimate cause of any mental disorder was the sinful behavior of the patient. First came debauchery and dissoluteness; then came domestic strife, poverty, loss of wealth, neglected education, unhappiness in love, jealousy, shock, wounded pride, homesickness (especially among the Swiss), disappointment, deaths, political happenings, excessive study, vehement play, piety carried to excess, guilty conscience, obstinacy, inactivity and disinterest in a productive life, whimsical and luxurious living, ambition, vanity, anger, conflicting religious beliefs, superstition and repressed emotions. Grossly exaggerating the facts, Ideler said of disappointment in love: "Unless we can read a woman's heart and appreciate the frightful role played by disappointment, jealousy and vanity, we shall always be baffled by the recalcitrant and often fatal illnesses which they engender: menstrual disorders, a host of mental diseases, and finally diverse forms of fatal consumptive afflictions. Homesickness, according to Neumann, might produce the same results: "When it does not culminate in suicide, it kills through consumptive fever. Once fever sets in, we can be certain that death will follow unless the patient returns to his home. If he does, he will recover immediately from his homesickness." Guislain associated suicide and homesickness with inflammation of intestines and even attributed the high incidence of intestinal disorder among patients in insane asylums to homesickness resulting from their confinement. In keeping with the orientation of his age, he was prone to regard sympathetic diseases of the digestive system and lungs as by-products of insanity. Blumröder also spoke of a "reciprocal connection between cause and effect. Biased thinking creates spurious images in the brain, and spurious images in the brain create biased, unsound thinking. Persistent dread entails mollification of the brain, and through mollification of the brain patients become downcast and timorous. Violent anger fills the head with blood and stimulates the liver; inversely, head congestion and liver irritation provoke anger."

Oddly enough, excessive elation was designated as a cause of insanity. Rush, for example, cited cases in which insanity developed as a consequence of winning the grand prize in a lottery, of an unusually remunerative career or of a happy marriage; and Arnold, quoting Hale (a doctor who worked in Bedlam), reported that of all those who became insane as a result of their affiliation with the South Sea Company in 1720, the incalculably rich by far outnumbered the poor. Hoffbauer found this "both natural and noteworthy ... The man who suddenly finds that he has reached his goal thinks that he no longer has to weigh and deal with the issues that have heretofore guided his steps but can give free reign to his imagination. The relaxation of judgment soon culminates in insanity." By contrast, a man who suffers a sudden reversal is either forced to initiate "cool, calm deliberation" or totally deprived of the faculty for deliberation. If he loses this faculty, he at first becomes downcast and despondent, then foolish and imbecile. Horn cited another danger posed by favorable circumstances: "Many lose their reason because they have had too much happiness and have been spoiled to such a degree that they are unable to bear up under or to rise above the petty sufferings which are part and parcel of human existence." Still others become sick "because they lived in idleness and sloth" or "because their occupations were unchallenging, made too few demands on them, or gave too much encouragement to a morbifically active imagination."

Fear of the consequences of mental strain, still widespread today, was voiced in a statement by Cox to the effect that "deep, persistent thinking" tended to weaken, bewilder, and destroy the intellect. "If persistent, penetrating thinking is often practiced," wrote Willis, "if the brain is repeatedly overstimulated and abused, then this sickly condition becomes permanent; material changes occur in the brain; the intellect is thrown into confusion." Hoffbauer also held that "just a single instance of putting excessive strain on the imagination can cause madness," so "prolonged strain can increase the danger of madness."

François de Mesmer, founder of the animal magnetism theory, applying it here to the sick.

That would explain why musicians, artists, and poets were more likely than others to fall prey to insanity. He cited Pinel's remark concerning patients in the Bicetre. There were among them no men "who constantly used their intellect," and therefore no natural scientists, no capable physicists, no chemists, and but few clerics. Vering considered the study of abstract sciences dangerous. Rush called attention to the fact that among those most likely to become mentally ill were men bent on discovering the secret of perpetual motion, finding the philosopher's stone, or interpreting the prophecies in the Bible. He also believed that insanity could easily result from overtaxing the memory, from jumping frequently and hastily from one subject to another as booksellers must do, or from straining the imagination (as poets do) constantly over a protracted period.

Similarly, Muller and Vering held that women frequently became insane as a result of reading novels too zealously. "Bad novels have perverted the minds of many of these unfortunate women," wrote the latter. "They have irreparably corrupted their behavior and stifled their zest for life." Blumroder believed that many people were driven insane by dreams, especially if their dreams were repeated.

Here symptoms of the disease were obviously mistaken for the cause. This was clearly the case when Heinroth traced megalomania back to pride and when he not infrequently attributed melancholia to remorse over earlier short-comings. "When the best years of life are over," he wrote, "and when vital energy is spent, how can life be shaped anew? A man then needs above all else to acquire a new taste for life. If he fails at the outset and surrenders, he has taken the first step toward melancholia, the awful hell from which all too often there is no escape."

mental/physical hypothesis

Opinions concerning the relation of mental causes of insanity to physical causes differed markedly, depending on the position taken by the individual with respect to the basic issue of psychic versus somatic medicine. Guislain classed as psychic causes those "that infringe upon our basic needs and most intimate feelings." By far the strongest morbific forces, they accounted for five out of six cases of insanity. Noting that these mental disorders were often characterized initially by a feeling of dejection, he concluded that they were caused by mental suffering. Summarizing his own observations, Esquirol attributed insanity to psychic influences in 681 instances, to physical causes in 367 instances, and to hereditary factors in 337 instances. Singled out as physical causes were onanism, excessive application of quicksilver, misuse of spirits (but apparently not to so great an extent then as now), sunstroke, blows on the head, brain disorders, cholera, childbed, and constipation.

One conviction then widely held—and one that continually reappears in certain writings today—was that onanism entailed dire consequences. The terrifying details were depicted in the worst possible light by Tissot, Chiarugi, Oegg, Zeller, Haindorf, and others. Then chronic illness, imbecility, dessication of the spinal marrow, paralysis, and death were believed to result from onanism; today, however, we know that while onanism may sometimes result from mental disorders, it can never cause them. Both repression of the sex drive and promiscuity were also posited as causes of insanity.

A theory of crises then held sway in medicine. Along with this theory went the view, commonly held by older alienists, that the secretion of saliva or tears, cutaneous eruptions, perspiration, vomiting, and evacuation often effected "critical" cures by ejecting harmful substances from the body of the mental patient; and conversely, that the absence of such processes could entail insanity. Blockage of perspiration or lactation, absence of menstrual flow or menstruation, bleeding from hemorrhoids or nostrils, disappearance of cutaneous eruptions, desiccation of ulcers, shifting of rheumatic or arthritic pains from peripheral areas to vital inner organs, and precipitous scabbing were all regarded with suspicion and credited with being of fundamental significance in the development of mental illness. Guislain described a case in which meningitis supposedly resulted from delousing. Frequently cases were cited in which a physical disorder alternated with a psychic disturbance.

Another category of causes, as vast as it was vague, involved enteric conditions, inflammations, dislocation of the viscera (generally the large intestine), blockage of the portal veins, accumulation of worms in the intestines, pain in the solar plexis, hepatic atony, excessive discharge of bile, plethora of the spleen and diseases of the kidneys, pancreas or sex organs. Rush cited cases in which mental disorders were brought on by the smell of lead or other minerals. Still others posited changes in air pressure, the seasons and the phases of the moon as influences on the development of insanity.

That much confusion pervaded the thinking of observers is evident from one of Esquirol's contributions. He stated that he had seen how insanity could be brought on by "living in a new house, washing the head with cold water, squeezing a pimple, catching a head cold, remission of rheumatic and arthritic pains and eradication of herpetic eruption." As other causative conditions he cited irregularities in the menstrual cycle, old age, child bed, a blow on the head, senility, high fever, shrinkage of hemorrhoids, constipation, syphilis, misuse of mercury, disorderly behavior, excessive drinking, onanism, disappointment in love, shock, political upheavals, thwarted ambition, excessive study or mental activities, poverty, domestic troubles, delirium, melancholia, epilepsy, paralysis, apoplexy, strenuous, exhausting activities and even blood-letting.

The exact nature of the relation of these and many other causes of illnesses to specific types of mental disturbances was as a rule vague. Bergmann, however, tried to relate mania and *melancholia mesenterica* to the gastric nerves, and Autenrieth believed that he had identified one type of epilepsy that originated in the navel. Sauvage designated as *daemonomania polonica* madness assumed to develop as a result of cutting off or being unable to loosen a Polish plait (elf-lock).

We note in passing that belief in demoniacal possession, which had played such an important role in trials for witchcraft, had still not been completely eradicated. Heinroth's assertion that the madman's soul mated with evil is to be interpreted metaphorically, but Kerner and Eschenmayer, deluded by the symptoms of hysterical women, thought that they must attribute derangement to physical suffering and the latter to demoniacal possession. Kerner compared the symptoms of possession and of madness. He prescribed as the sole remedy for the former the Holy Word and the name of Jesus. "It is reasonable to assume," he explained in 1835, "that if a Messiah and worker of miracles or a real Magus entered one of our asylums, among a number of incurable lunatics he would also discover some patients who are truly possessed and whom he could cure, either by adjuration in the name of Jesus or with the help of physical instruments. The same holds true for epilepsy." This view was still defended in theological writings even during the second half of the nineteenth century. On various occasions I myself in recent years have known of cases in which mental patients were treated with holy water and exorcized on being admitted to the institution.

Behavior of patients was generally considered first in attempts to type mental disorders. The great botanist Linnaeus had already used his system to classify mental disorders, just as he had previously classified plants and animals, according to genus, species and subspecies. Chiarugi attempted a similar classification. He identified three genera (melancholia, mania, and imbecility), each subdivided into a series of species and countless subspecies. Subdivisions were based partly on the severity of the disease and its symptoms; partly on the patient's rationality, mood and conduct; and partly on a plethora of presumed causes associated with as many types of disorders. Using the same general plan, Flemming later divided the "family of psychic disturbances (amentiae)" into two main groups and these groups into a great number of classes and subclasses; sometimes he took as his criterion the severity, nature or progress of the disease; occasionally, however, he fell back upon its cause.

Most researchers were satisfied with a number of simple classes which mirrored only the most obvious differences. Esquirol, for example, made a distinction between melancholia and monomania accompanied by circumscribed moods—the former by sadness and the latter by cheerfulness—and established as separate categories mania accompanied by delirium and agitation, derangement accompanied by want of clarity and the inability to reason, and imbecility or cretinism. Kant identified folly (amentia), insanity (dementia), and silliness (vesania). Oegg made a distinction between mania or delirium, imbecility, and lunacy or madness (including melancholia). Classification was generally based on an assessment of psychic faculties and, after that, on evidence relating to depression or exaltation. Thus Heinroth classed madness as exaltation of mood, lunacy as exaltation of the power of imagination, and frenzy as exaltation of the will power; he used the corresponding forms of depression to classify melancholia, imbecility, and want of will power. Groos had recourse to a similar tripartition based on the Platonic idea of the direct relation between brain and imagination, breast and feelings, bowels and desire; but he created a fourth classification by adding to each of the primary groups the element of exaltation or depression (mania in contrast to congenital imbecility). Buzorini similarly designated disorders of the imaginative faculty as *vesaniae encephalopathicae*, those of the senses as *vesaniae gangliothoracicae*, and those of the passions as *vesaniae ganglioabdominales;* the last, mixed group he named *vesaniae encephalo-gangliopathicae*.

Jacobi was still following the same route in 1844 when he divided into contrasting groups disorders affecting the passions and those affecting the intellect. Frenzy and depression, for instance, stood in contrast to madness and imbecility. But the addition of the element of exaltation or depression resulted in mixed types, such as delirium and folly. In individual cases the most conspicuous characteristics provided the basis for countless refinements in terminology: *melancholia errabunda, misanthropica silvestris, anglica, hypochondrica, religiosa,* or *catholico: erotomania, daemonomania, metromania; mania ekstati ca, moria maniaca,* etc. Heinroth subdivided lunacy into derangement, madness, silliness and folly, depending on whether the disorder extended to ideas about everything, about objects or relationships in the material world, abstractions, or the individual himself.

If the nature of the illness was obscure, remedies suggested were as a rule all the more numerous. "The abundance of remedies for certain illnesses," said Damerow, "stems from the poverty and plight of our science." The same applied to the treatment of mental disturbances a century ago. In 1864 Schneider compiled a 600-page book solely on the subject of methods of treating mental disorders, and in 1803 Reil wrote more than 500 pages on the application of psychic therapy to mental disorders. Records indicate that doctors outdid themselves in writing outlandish prescriptions, mainly for the reason that they tended to see a causal relation between their favorite influences and the resulting symptoms. Doctors then assumed that if what they classed as insanity could result from almost any conceivable mishap, then it could probably be cured through medical intervention, an appropriately selected remedy, a brilliant exposition, or any one of the measures then subsumed under the designation of direct or indirect psychic therapy.

They were never able to decide whether the course of insanity was determined mainly by the basic pattern of the disorder or by external events. Mahir, for example, noted that Riedl gave painstaking consideration to delirium "since the slightest mistake in treating the disease might render it incurable." Guislain and his translator Zeller explained that an untimely blood-letting might cause a patient suffering from melancholia to become delirious or imbecile. "A single mishandling of a paroxys-

Drastic therapy around 1800. Fifty to a hundred pails of ice-cold water are poured on the patient. Below, left: Whirling chair capable of a hundred turns a minute. Below, right: Patient wearing wire mask.

mal patient," said Oegg (and Blumröder concurred), "can mean the difference between recovery and incurability." Similarly Neumann held that a cold bath could occasion the transformation of mania into imbecility, and that the "otherwise apparently useless" swing devised by Cox (to be discussed later) might ward off this danger. "If lunatics seldom recover through treatment," he confidently explained, "the guilt lies in the profession or in the practitioner as frequently as in the affliction itself." His attitude is reflected today in that of people who attribute the plight of their relatives to all sorts of adverse circumstances or improper measures, but mainly to presumed blunders on part of the physician. The conditions that obtained in the case of one doctor or of one institution with a record of successes were often posited as ideal for the treatment of all patients; these successes were actually attributable mainly to the condition of the patients who were admitted for treatment. The same line of reasoning also applies to the widespread belief in the efficacy of "crises." It was hoped that artificially induced crises would have a decisive influence on the progress of the disease. Guislain himself looked upon the pressure bandage as a device for collecting serum in the brain cavity and assumed that a copious flow of pus from infected wounds signified improvement in the activity of the brain.

Emetics and purgatives played a dominant role in the treatment of insanity. Schneider used no fewer than 34 emetics and at least 50 purgatives, excluding mineral waters, all of which were prescribed in many different proportions. Emetics were supposed to convulse the patient and in this way to stimulate the nerves in the abdominal region and heighten the activity of various organs; to rid the stomach and upper enteron of mucus, bile, undigested food, poison, acids and other harmful substances; and finally, to calm or excite certain nerve centers "antagonistically" by inducing nausea. Its close relation to the stomach was supposed to make possible a sympathetic reaction in the brain. The "nausea treatment" was then accorded primary importance because of its presumed efficacy in putting an end to riotous practices motivated by the unbridled selfishness that was alleged to have led to the patient's insanity. "Its violent effects are felt by even the most obtuse imbecile," wrote Vering. Because of its soothing effect, Neumann found it most efficacious in the case of agitated, unruly patients. "In such a psychic state," explained Schneider, "whether we are dealing with mania, melancholia, or moria, we can take for granted that the subjective personality is figuratively destroyed and that the psyche, freed from its physical husk and wafted to a higher plain, no longer recognizes its own personality. But nausea as well as repeated applications of emetics and purgatives introduces into the material organism a new sickness which is communicated to the whole sensorium directly through the plexus of nerves in the stomach and through the whole network of nerves in the abdominal region. But since the psyche always maintains certain ties with its material substratum, it is compelled to descend from its ethereal perch and to re-enter its husk and examine the changes that might have occurred in its absence. This act of reflecting is the *ancora sacra* of the distinct personality that makes its reappearance; the longer nausea persists, the more attentive the psyche becomes to the strange new process; it widens the gap between the psyche and its transcendal perch and brings into clearer focus the consciousness of the returning personality; sustained nausea prevents the mental patient from becoming immersed in his own thoughts."

Schneider extolled especially the virtues of ipecacuanha. He observed that delirious patients after drinking one or more glasses of ipecacuanha tea "became remarkably calm and cheerful. It was as if some incomprehensible power had caused the psyche, previously wrenched loose from its husk, once again to form a harmonious union with the body."

The administering of purgatives was dictated mainly by the causal links presumed to exist between insanity and disorders of the abdominal region, namely those of liver, intestines, and solar plexus. Purgatives were supposed to eliminate "infarcts and crudities," exert a favorable influence on the vascular system and the nervous system, and rid the head of congestion. Here it was also assumed that his physical distress and the phenomena that accompanied it would distract the patient's attention from his musings and focus it on his physical condition. Tobacco smoke was administered in the form of an enema by a special machine in severe cases of imbecility and *melancholia attonita*, which were attributed to a sickly condition engendered by either sluggishness or constipation. The hellebore root, highly prized by the ancients as a remedy for mental disorders, was supposed to do away with abdominal plethora, re-establish the menstrual cycle, remove "atribilious impurities" and eliminate intestinal blocks. In the same way, quicksilver was used to stimulate the flow of saliva. Schneider held that because of the close relation between the salivary glands and the genitalia, quicksilver could be put to good use in the treatment of melancholia resulting from disappointment in love.

Except for henbane, cherry laurel, belladonna, aconite and opium (which had been recommended by Chiarugi for treating melancholia), relatively little use was made of narcotic agents. Guislain adopted the view held by Mahir and warned that these drugs might cause incurable paralysis. Soporific drugs, by and large relatively recent chemical discoveries, were not then available. Stimulants and cordials were extensively employed; prescribed in addition to volatile oils, teas and roots were camphor, valerian, musk, castoreum, Spanish fly, phosphorus, ether, spirits of wine and ammonia.

Consonant with the prevalent medical beliefs was the use of skin irritants and diversionary agents. Mustard plasters and blisters on the head and neck were supposed to cause a transformation or "metaschematism" of the disorder by checking perspiration, driving arthritic pains inward, and curdling milk. Salves were also rubbed into pustules on the top of the head to produce the same effect. This treatment, highly prized by many even though rejected outright by others, entailed severe irritation, scaling and mortification of the scalp until it "looked like a nightcap"—even decay of the bones of the skull and mutilation of the genital organs since patients often aggravated their sores by rubbing them and in this way transferred some of the salve to other areas of the body. "The suffering that attends the formation of these pustules is often indescribable," observed Schneider. He expressed the hope, along with Horn, that continuous suffering would enable the patient "to regain consciousness of his true self, to wake from his supersensual slumber and to stay awake." Similar effects were achieved by using ants or scabies to force the patient lost in the world of his imagination to adopt a new train of thought. Scourging with stinging *treating the physical with a view of effecting the psyche.*

nettles produced "gratifying results" in the case of patients who were lazy, deceitful, mean, stubborn, or elusive, or who showed suicidal tendencies. Finally, we should also mention setons (which, according to Neumann, could transport the patient from the world of his dreams to the world of reality) and fontanels, dry cupping-glasses, incisions in the skin, and red-hot irons, all of which were often used for diversionary purposes. Heat was applied simultaneously to the crown of the head and the soles of the feet. "The pain inflicted in this way defies description," wrote Schneider. Pienitz recommended irritation of the skin for chronic delirious patients when their behavior became "too inflexible and presumptuous."

Another major weapon in the arsenal of the older alienists was blood-letting, which was supposed not only to rid the brain of excess blood but also to exert a favorable influence on its condition. Rush extolled the practice and reported that in one instance he had successfully administered 47 blood-lettings over a period of 11 months. It was then common knowledge, however, that many mental patients evidenced a lack of blood rather than an excess. The indiscriminate and unreasonable practice of blood-letting was therefore condemned by many alienists. Esquirol wrote disparagingly of a patient who in 48 hours had been bled 13 times. Pinel observed that there was some doubt as to who was more insane, the one who ordered the blood-letting or the one subjected to the practice. Guislain declared that one untimely or excessive blood-letting could lead to incurable insanity. To prevent coagulation in the nose, hemorrhoidal vein or genitalia, practitioners put leeches and bloody cupping-glasses on the forehead, nose, neck, buttock or abdomen. Parry sought to repress delirium by compressing the jugular vein, and Bird even proposed the application of a ligature. Occasionally transfusion of animal blood was also proposed or at least discussed. Heinroth entertained the hope that in cases in which vital energy had been depleted, a new stream of energizing blood might revitalize the brain and nerves. Chiarugi recommended that this "irrational and dangerous device" be outlawed.

The notion that disturbed patients ought not to eat too heartily was apparently widespread. Many doctors rightly understood that debilitation was often responsible for agitation, yet there was a tendency to include emetics and purgatives in rich, refreshing liquids or in gruel; many patients were also denied meals for "improper" behavior. Vering held that deprivation of food and drink for long periods had a salubrious effect on the patient. For disciplinary purposes Heinroth recommended, along with the use of restraints, deprivation of food, water and sleep. It seems unlikely, however, that he ever actually used to any great extent the inhuman treatment that he described.

Baths were used in diverse ways. Sudden immersion in cold water—the *bain de surprise*—was to induce massive shivering and an appropriate reaction. This was supposed "though a violent shock" to break the chain of delusory ideas and perhaps create conditions favoring sane thinking. In addition, it apparently inspired fear in patients "stubbornly opposed to the use of medications or determined not to submit to rules established for the common good." In one instance, after a patient had supposedly responded favorably to immersion in a pool, it was decided to hold her under the water at the risk of drowning her "as long as it took to recite the Miserere." Richard recommended dashing cold water into the patient's face.

He thought that by focusing his attention on the water and on the person administering it, he could condition the delirious patient in such a way as to make him correct his short-comings. In keeping with the laws of thought association, the sight of water was supposed to "remind the patient that improper conduct would lead to punishment." Simliar considerations led Rush to recommend pouring cold water down the sleeves.

Shower-baths were also employed. In Juliusspital water was poured from a height of 20 feet into a funnel-shaped basket above the patient's head. Schneider devised a mechanism for showering cold water down on a patient at will and collecting it in a large container. He surmised that this contrivance "would prove to be most helpful in the treatment of insanity." Langermann complained in a report in 1804 that his institution (St. George) had no ducking pen. He reported that the emotional shock entailed by an unexpected plunge into cold water and the resulting fear of a repetition of the terrifying experience could cause patients who could be diverted in no other way from their irrational behavior to make an attempt to behave rationally. The patient was plunged suddenly into the water when he responded to the challenge to walk across a bridge and into an inviting summerhouse.

Drenchings were also administered in certain instances. From an imposing height 10—or even 40 or 50—buckets of water were dashed "rather forcibly" on the head of the patient suffering from delusion. This treatment was used for severe forms of melancholia and hypochondria (including agitation, rage and constipation), as well as for the patient with a dissolute past—one who had been addicted to drinking strong wine or accustomed to sumptuous eating. Horn heaped praise on this treatment and surmised that it had cured a number of mental patients whose plight otherwise would have remained hopeless: "It calms and soothes the insane; it cools heads made feverish by congestion of the blood; it makes unruly patients docile and orderly; it enables the dumb to speak; it changes the outlook of those bent on self-destruction; it awakens self-consciousness in the motionless melancholiac obsessed by his brooding; it has a salubrious effect on imbecile patients; and in many instances it contributes to the maintenance of calm and order in its role as an instrument for shocking and punishing patients." Against this, Amerlung stated that he had not found drenchings very useful but on the contrary had frequently observed that they affected patients adversely: "As a rule patients later became more restless, more delirious, and more confused than before, although they had been calmer just after the treatment." Pienitz rarely employed drenching, and never "without a certain ritual exhortation and admonition." Jacobi complained that in one institution for several successive weeks, up to 300 buckets of cold water were dashed forcibly down on a patient's head.

'When the douche was administered, the patient was first immobilized, then a strong jet of icy water was sprayed by a portable fire extinguisher on his head, neck or shoulders. It served also as a "corrective device in the case of stubborn, mean, intractable lunatics." It induced them "to submit to the established rules." They were sorely afraid of this mechanism; indeed, "the mere threat that it might be used was often enough to accomplish the desired end." In one variation of this practice, thin stream of cold water was allowed to fall a considerable distance from a small spout to a certain spot on the patient's skull. "The sensation gradually elicited by this device,"

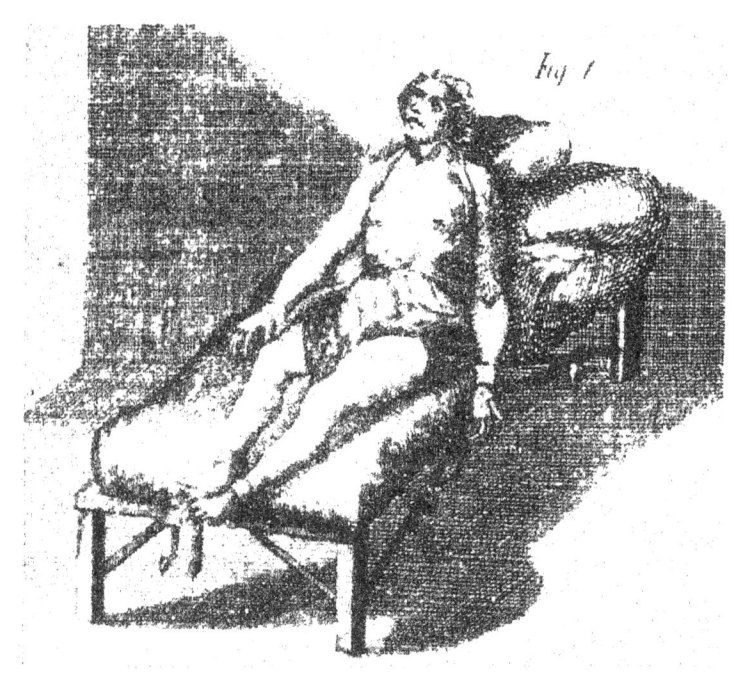

A chained psychotic

said Schneider, "is often unbearable. In former times this painful device was used as a mild form of torture in punishing criminals." He added that he used the device "for persistent, violent, nervous headaches or for sleeplessness resulting from acute head congestions." Jacobi reported that he had seen the stream of water break the skin within a few minutes and bloodily tear away the fragments. Exposure to the rain was less painful. Hot water was occasionally poured on the patient's head, but this always entailed the possibility of scalding his face and ears.

Though we may question today the practice of subjecting patients to barbarous treatment, we must commend the older alienists for promoting hot baths. They hoped that hot baths would help to solve the problems created by uncleanliness, increase perspiration (the reverse was assumed to be the cause of melancholia) and again bring to the surface repressed cutaneous eruptions (their reappearance was assumed to contribute to recovery). The older alienists also emphasized their sleep-inducing effect and the soothing influence that they generally exerted on weak, depressed patients. Tuke stated that warm baths were more important and more effective than any medication in treating most cases of melancholia. "In the case of a frail female patient whose body has been debilitated for any one of a number of reasons," said Cox, "the warm bath has a remarkable power to calm the turbulence that rages in her mind and body even after she has become violent, dangerous, and stubbornly opposed to internal medication." Mitivié lengthened the duration of the bath to as many as 6 or 8 hours, depending on the patient's restlessness and unruliness. Simultaneous cooling of the patient's head was also frequently recommended. The difficulty of holding restless, resistant patients in the bath was met by a device still employed to a limited extent—a tub equipped with a lid which allowed only the patient's head to protrude. Since water often spilled out, Heyner put a funnel-like container around the patient's head.

Salt was added to the bathwater to further stimulate the skin. Schneider even recommended mustard baths, especially for sly, restless, evasive, brooding or phlegmatic mental patients. Curiously, Cox prescribed baths in thin gruel or in water and milk, and Schneider baths in gravy for patients who refused their food.

Inevitably, two new discoveries, electricity and galvanism, were used experimentally in the treatment of mental patients, particularly since many nervous disorders were believed to entail an unhealthy accumulation of nervous or electrical fluids in the brain. The most diverse procedures were employed—electrified currents of air, electrical air-baths, condensation, electrical shocks, and galvanization. Gall had correlated areas of the brain and mental faculties; Schneider thought that through polar treatment he could influence different areas of the brain. Researchers went so far as to conclude that if treatment from one pole intensified suffering, a reversal of the pole would bring relief.

Animal magnetism, though occasionally used in the treatment of mental patients, was considered a degenerate form of electricity. Its most enthusiastic advocate was Haindorf, who looked upon it as "man's best weapon against disease" and attributed to it the possibility of "presentiment and prophecy." Heinroth, who called it "a wild branch of religious faith" and rightly realized that the hypnotist's will played a vital role in it, went one step further and discussed the possibility of influencing psychic disorders directly through the credulous will. "If an unclean mind can corrupt a clean one," he reasoned, "then a healthy, divinely-inspired mind can heal an unhealthy one." He believed in the possibility of a spiritual contact or a direct psychical influence through the higher faith of the clean mind even though this was normally ruled out by restraints imposed on the human will. He noted that others would charge that he was irresponsible and irrational, but that his hypothesis could be verified or refuted only on the basis of objective experimentation; he added that the preliminary conditions required for such an experiment could hardly be established.

As the last examples show, medical treatment alone would not satisfy the older alienists. "It is a revolting spectacle," acidly wrote Reil, "to see a brash empiric cavorting with his mental patient. Like a blind mole he burrows into his intestines and searches for the soul in the region where nature placed the equipment for carrying out our animal functions. He tries to correct mental aberrations by thinning atrabilious blood or by liquifying coagulated humors in the portal veins, and to combat psychic suffering with helebore and psychic confusion with syringes. Woe unto the image of God who falls into such hands!" Neumann expressed his views in similar fashion: "The time has finally come for us to stop looking for the herb or salt or metal which in homeopathic or allopathic doses will cure mania, imbecility, insanity, fury or passion. They will never be found until pills are discovered which will transform a naughty child into a well-mannered child, an ignorant man into a skilled artist, a rude swain into a polished gentleman. We can rub patients with martyr's ointment until the skin peels off and turn up more martyrs than the Spanish Inquisition—and still face the fact that we are not one step closer to curing insanity. Man's psychic activities are changed, not by medicines but by habit, training and exertion." And Conolly dryly observed: "It would seem that those who repeatedly extol the merits of a long list of drugs should at least have the opportunity to test in large institutions the items in which they have the greatest confidence."

Many practices, though purportedly medical practices, were intended primarily or at least occasionally to influence the inner life, and this generally by engendering fear. Since doctors—even those who conceded the importance of physical causes of insanity—could not free themselves outright from the views according to which we ordinarily pass judgment on others, they inferred from their behavior that many patients were foolish, absurd, wicked, malicious, stubborn, insubordinate and insolent, and they attempted to reform them by resorting to the methods used to discipline children. Neumann concluded his remarks (see above) with this sentence: "The mental patient must be handled like an ill-behaved child, and the measures used to correct the child can also be used to advantage with the lunatic." A similar opinion was voiced by Autenrieth: "The doctor can never sufficiently impress upon himself and others the fact that the insane are identical in most respects to stubborn, ill-mannered children and, like them, require stern (not cruel) treatment." Pinel also held that patients ought to be treated like children who, because they have a superabundance of energy, may resort to dangerous practices. Willis compared them to obstinate, unruly children who, convinced that they know more than their parents and their nurses, never follow instructions but always take pleasure in doing what is prohibited. Langermann recommended study of the precepts, measures, and skills used by educators to mold infantile minds—to stir, exercise and shape their conduct. Hoffbauer looked upon the rehabilitation of a madman who had regained his sanity as a second education of the same man. "Its not the treatment of mental patients frequently comparable to education of children?" asked Heinroth. And he continued: "Every finding indicates that the comparison is apt."

"Respect and love for his parents and teachers," concluded Vering, "and fear of punishment for wrong-doings are the primary agents that compel the child to be submissive and obedient. The collective experience of alienists proves that the same emotions are equally effective in exacting obedience and submissiveness from lunatics but that they can be aroused only by truly fatherly treatment on the part of the doctor. Reason and experience also show beyond doubt that the doctor's conduct in the presence of lunatics ought generally to be similar to that practiced by a wise and loving father in rearing his children." His essential characteristics would therefore be manly sternness and dignity, loving-kindness and benevolence, conscientiousness and sympathy, and justice tempered by mercy.

Attempts were made to influence patients through arguments founded on reason and through persuasion. The doctor ought therefore according to Reil to eschew all high-sounding words and to express his ideas and his reasoning so clearly and plainly that they could be grasped by the simplest mind. He should either convince the deluded patient of the futility of his course or rid him of his delusion by inculcating new ideas. Since ordinary experience showed that such words generally fell on deaf ears, however, the doctor was advised first to win the patient's confidence by adopting his viewpoint and then to persuade him to give up his particular objective. For instance, the doctor might pretend (as Chiarugi suggested) to believe that the patient's delusion was real and then recommend a remedy. It was assumed that one could right the intellect by attacking at the point where intellectual activity seemed to have gone astray; a trenchant remark at the appropriate time might bring a patient to his senses. Countless deceits were practiced to convince the lunatic of the falsity of his notions. To the melancholiac ob-obsessed by sin, divine absolution was imparted ceremoniously or during a mock trial, perhaps with the assistance of an angel who miraculously appeared. Cox attempted to rid patients of delusions by using phosphorous to flash "supernatural" messages on a screen.

Hypochondriacal disorders were corrected through sham operations during which the object presumed to have caused the difficulty—perhaps a snake or a lizard—was ostensibly removed from the body and exhibited to the patient. Jacobi reported the example of a patient in the Wurtzburg hospital who suffered from the illusion that someone inside his abdomen was talking to him. After a thick vesicant had been placed on the patient's abdomen and left there a sufficient time, the surgeon made an incision and pretended to remove the troublesome creature (actually an obstetrical manekin secretly brought along for the occasion) from the lunatic's body and to banish him immediately. The deception was remarkably effective. The patient's boundless joy over his deliverance was immediately apparent." A few minutes later, however, his umbilical cord reminded him that another such creature must have been left in his belly, and this time the imaginary creature did not disappear. Organs which seemed to the patient to be misplaced or lost were brought palpably to his attention. A series of such cures was reported in the form of expurgated anecdotes. They were all alike in that, as we have already remarked, the deluded patient always displayed extraordinary ingenuity and often succeeded in outwitting the doctor. It was always possible to convince the patient that he had been freed from evil but not that he had been harassed by a figment of his imagination.

Attempts were also made to influence the emotions of patients. Damerow stated that anything capable of influencing the psychic life and causing insanity could also be looked upon as a remedy. He therefore correlated different emotional states with different drugs—joy with valerian (or at higher levels opium and wine), cheerfulness with stimulants, fear with sedatives and salty substances, anger with essential oils and phosphorous, rage with ipecacuanha, shock with narcotics, nux vomica and belladonna. He recommended studies to determine the correct manner of administering these psychic poisons and of effecting their gradual withdrawal. Haindorf recommended that emotions antithetical to these responsible for the disorder be used in treating melancholia.

Much attention was given to attempts to counteract, restrain and mollify by force the symptoms of the insane. "The outrages practiced by brutal, self-centered, ambitious, proud, lustful, arrogant, vain, vindictive and envious patients can be controlled and corrected only through humiliation, shame and contempt," according to Schneider. Lunatics who suffered from *melancholia metamorphosis* (which reflected a change in their social position and personality) were to be deeply humiliated in order that they might be made to feel more acutely their worthlessness and dependency. Hoffbauer, who once condemned the use of brutality against patients, condoned as educationally sound Willis' policy of permitting attendants to strike back at offending patients. For repressing arrogance or eliminating excessive pride Esquirol recommended that patients be made acutely aware of their plight. To a patient who was always heaping abuse upon himself and others Heinroth administered an admonition followed by a smart slap in the face; this kept her within the bounds of propriety and from that moment on gave him such strict control over her that she submitted blindly to his instructions. Haslam held that the superintendent of an asylum ought to possess a strong character, be able to gain the respect of patients, and know how when the occasion arose decisively to assert his authority. "He must seldom use threats, but when he does, he must execute them; if a patient refuses to obey him, he must unhesitatingly mete out punishment. If the madman is strong and energetic, the superintendent must call other men to help him in order to instill fear in the patient and exact swift obedience without having to exert or endanger himself. Autenrieth declared that a "breaking of the will" or a penetration into the will of the patient, was a necessary part of any complete cure.

—Even Pinel believed that one of the most effective means of treating insanity was "to subdue the patient and to tame him, as it were, by making him dependent on a man who by virtue of his moral and physical qualities can dominate him and change his aberrant pattern of thinking." Patients ought to be imbued with a sense of urgency. "They soon understand that they must immediately submit to whatever is required of them, that the doctor's will is for them a strict and unchangeable law. After they have had this notion impressed upon them vividly and frequently in different ways, then they are no more likely

J. E D. Esquirol

to rebel against his will than against the laws of nature." The doctor ought therefore, above all else, to impress the patient forcibly. As a shining example he cited Willis, an English doctor who had formerly been a clergyman: "His face, usually friendly and affable, changes completely its character the moment he catches sight of one of his patients. It undergoes a metamorphosis instantaneously and commands the attention and respect of the madman. Penetrating eyes seem to read his heart and to divine his thoughts as soon as they come into being. Over them he exercises something resembling sovereign authority, which subsequently becomes a therapeutic instrument and which in no way contravenes the employment of gentler instruments." The main requirement for effecting a cure, according to Haindorf, was the ability of the doctor to impress the patient through his appearance in such a way as to compel obedience without instilling fear. "He must have sufficient control over his physiognomy to convey his intention to the patient by a glance. According to circumstances, in his face seriousness must alternate with pleasantry, benevolence with harshness, friendliness and love with contempt and complete scorn; his countenance must clearly reflect his will." Rush explained that the doctor's first step on entering a cell was to catch the patient's eye and disarm him with a look. The same technique was used by Pargeter, while Heinroth and Roller both prescribed a blend of harshness and tenderness. According to Heinroth the doctor ought to seem like a helper and savior, father and benefactor, compassionate friend and friendly teacher—but also like an exacting adminstrator of justice and a visible image of God; and he ought to conduct himself in the manner of a monarch. "Institutional regulations and instructions seem like inexorable decrees handed down by *Deus omnipotens;* he is the personification of both harshness and tenderness. In his first role, he rebuffs recalcitrant patients; in his second, he welcomes those who are docile. In his first role he metes out punishments and in his second, rewards. In his first role, he installs in the minds of the insane fear and obedience; in his second he inspires love and trust." Vering explained that "the doctor's command must be stated seriously and forcefully and must be delivered in an imperious tone and with an imperious mien if even his superficial features are to express the strong, unyielding will of the doctor—his *sic volo, sic jubeo*—in an impressive manner. If the command is not obeyed, threats can be added. One can threaten with a thunderous voice, with an annoyed look or an angry countenance. A shattering *quos ego* forcefully delivered in the form of a threat is sufficient to put an end, at least momentarily, to the restlessness and savage behavior of the most rabid lunatic unless he is totally impervious to external stimuli."

Such notions led naturally to the attempt to control patients through a system of punishments and rewards. Pinel considered this one of the most valuable therapeutic instruments. The whole course of the treatment ought to be adapted to the patient's behavior. "Proud, droll lunatics," said Vering, "require nothing more than a plain room with the bare essentials. Melancholic, timorous, and pious lunatics need friendly surroundings—a bright room provided with a beautiful view and gay pictures depicting comical scenes or beautiful landscapes." "Humiliate the proud patient and make him acutely aware of his worthlessness and dependency; handle the droll, amorous lunatic sternly and harshly so that he is always afraid. Treat the melancholic, fearful, and pious madman gently and with forbearance." If the lunatic is recalcitrant, has a bad character, or evidences a strong tendency to misbehave, with the result that he can injure himself or others, vigilance must be redoubled and appropriate punishment for each misdeed must be meted out without delay."

According to Sonnenstein's system, disobedience and bad conduct ought to be punished severely. "Punishment ought to be meted out as speedily as possible following an investigation of the offense." Reil stated that since the insane were devoid of inner motivation, they had to be compelled to allow themselves to be influenced from without. He explained that the insane had to be trained in the same way as animals and children: "Rewards that bring pleasure and punishments that bring displeasure should be meted out in a proportion calculated to lead patients back to the path which is necessary and proper for them and which will cause them to be submissive and to practice strict obedience. He thought that people who misbehaved or were deceitful, malicious, disobedient or recalcitrant, and who at the same time were cognizant of their misconduct and of the purpose of the punishment to which they were being subjected, could be helped by corrective training. They ought, however, to be punished only at the direction of the superintendent and by a designated official; switches of bullwhips should be used, but never inordinately and cruelly or in a manner injurious to the health; punishment should never be meted out during an emotional outburst and should always be effected in the presence on others. Similarly, he reasoned that isolation, hunger, and defamation were important corrective measures. Conversely, patients ought to have their attention called to paragons of virtue drawn from ancient and modern history and to episodes in their own lives; where feasible, they should be brought into the presence of others who might praise their good behavior and criticize their foolish acts. He reported that Erhard had seen an asylum in which filthy patients were put atop posts. "This was effective," he said, "because they were terrified by this disgrace." In an anteroom frequently visited by patients in Hirsch's hospital a chart was posted showing why they had been punished. Leupoldt recommended that patients be confronted on solemn occasions with "a detailed report on their conduct during the past several months." Esquirol reported that the threat of sending the insane to the incurable ward soothed them like magic. He also felt that the douche was a good instrument for curbing rage, breaking a dangerous resolution or forcing a patient to obey.

These views naturally found support in the notion, championed by Heinroth and his school, that mental disease resulted from a moral transgression, from voluntary surrender to a life of sin. "Individuals subjected to the strictest control," Heinroth explained, "seek the very freedom that would be most detrimental to them. They are lawless and wholly devoid of reason. They can be brought back under control, however, only by law; and since law can have no other meaning for them, it must appear to them, mechanically, as the absence of freedom. Free will must adapt itself to necessity, and unbridled instinct must be forced back within its bounds whenever it tries to find expression. This can readily be accomplished by using painless fetters to restrict physical movement; and such restriction, as experience still teaches me each day, helps—and often suffices—to bring about reflection. For a patient can not experience relentless opposition without becoming aware of it; and awareness is the first step toward rational reflection. That is why I usually restrain patients who are ruled by their instincts (unless they are maniacs) until they submit to the will of the doctor. If the doctor possesses sufficient willpower to influence a patient directly from the outset or over a period of time, then he will not need to employ mechanical restraint; nothing can be accomplished without it, however, if the patient fails to respond to commands." Such considerations therefore resulted in the methodical immobilization of patients not, as previously, out of cruelty or out of fear of them, but for the purpose of setting them on the right course. A particular fault must always be punished in accordance with a specific rule, as Richard explained, if it was to be eradicated. Hayner held that strict punctuality in the application of punitive measures would spare the unfortunate sufferer many disagreeable and painful experience and that a stern, lengthy admonition to each new patient to conform to the rules of the institution would entail less frequent use of coercive and corrective instruments.

There was often disagreement concerning the doctor's role in meting out punishment. "The doctor in charge of the asylum must never try to instill fear in patients. He must have at his command an individual who can be charged with this unpleasant task, who will act only under his orders, and against whom the rage, anger, and violent outbursts of the insane can be directed in case of need." Neumann was even more explicit in stating that the doctor ought to appear to have no part in administering coercive measures "for if he appears to the patient as the author of his confinement, he loses not only the patient's trust but also all hope of ever helping him. Each asylum must have at least one attendant or other subordinate whom patients fear and who has the right to apply all necessary coercive measures." He ought, according to Guislain, to possess great physical strength, a forbidding appearance, a forceful voice, and a resolute character. It is hard to understand how a doctor could hope to resort to such deception and still retain the trust of his patients. Haindorf was more candid in requiring that all punishment be administered openly, in the presence of the doctor and several other patients, "to rule out any suspicion of injustice or cruelty that might otherwise spring up in the minds of other patients."

Isolation, or transfer to totally unfamiliar surroundings, was the prime weapon used to force the patient to surrender quickly and unconditionally to the doctor's will. "With but few exceptions," Georget affirmed, "we can say that patients do not recover in their own homes." Autenrieth was also of the opinion that in all probabilitty not one mental patient had recovered his sanity in familiar surroundings. Rush recommended that the patient be given a change of clothing, bedded down in a strange room, and superintended by strangers; nor should he have in his pockets anything that would remind him of his previous situation.

It was thought that the patient's past experiences would again evoke unhealthy ideas and reinforce his delusions. Haindorf even held that shame could cause a patient who had been reminded of the fact that he was once crazy to suffer a relapse into lunacy, and that God himself would then be unable to help him. He therefore stressed the necessity of arousing in the patient sensations that would break down his old pattern of thinking. Esquirol remarked that cures were effected more frequently among foreigners who came to Paris than among local inhabitants. Willis, who treated the queen of Portugal and George III of England, first changed living quarters, furnishings, and servants; his efforts in the first instance were wasted, supposedly because he did not procure a new confessor. He also observed that under the same circumstances foreigners responded more readily to the treatment than Englishmen because they were more completely isolated. Travel was recommended, as Chiarugi explained, for the purpose of distracting the imagination, even against the patient's will, and ridding the mind of unhealthy ideas through exposure to new surroundings. Visits by relatives and acquaintances were discouraged, and Roller advanced the theory in 1831 that such visits had an adverse influence on the insane: "A paroxysm or worsening of the illness ensues." We can be certain today that the carefully planned separation of the patient from his family, which seemed for a long time like "burying him alive" and putting him at the mercy of the doctor, was largely responsible for popular mistrust of asylums long after they had ceased to provide grounds for suspicion. Rumors concerning brutality in the old asylums were reinforced by the thick veil of secrecy that hid institutional life from the eyes of the masses.

We must give the old alienists credit for having exhibited both sincerity and inventiveness in putting into practice the therapeutic principles which they considered sound. Advice given by Neumann suggests the course of treatment that might have been prescribed for a new patient in a state of agitation: "They bring the patient to the restraining chair, bleed him, put ten or twelve leeches on his head, cover him with cold, wet towels, pour about fifty buckets of cold water over his head and let him eat thin soup, drink water and take Glauber salts." The same picture is suggested by Heinroth's account of the treatment for frenzied states: blood-letting to the point of syncope, repetition of the same process, administering cold showers, douching the head after it had been shaven, putting a crown of leeches around the head, sacrifying the skin and sprinkling cantharides in the open cuts, massaging with tartar salve, using tartar emetic to induce vomiting, applying belladonna, bayrum, gratiola or hellebore, and using the rack (to be discussed later) in certain instances to control rage.

A report of the Marsberg asylum for the year 1819 contains a detailed account of the coercive measures then practiced and recommendations for correcting the abuses that might result from their misuse. Mild coercion took the form of a diminution of food (until the patient was consuming only half the normal amount or until he suffered from malnutrition) and confinement in a dark room under the supervision of an attendant ostensibly indifferent toward the patient. Next came the English camisole or strait jacket, cotton cords for tying the patient's hands and buckles, straps and thongs for securing his limbs and fastening him to the bed; when worst came to worst the feet were also strapped together. The same objective was attained by sewing together the sleeves of a jacket buttoned on the back or the inside seams of ankle-length trousers. All these devices should be used "only under such psychological circumstances as (might be specified) by philosophers and doctors who have written from experience." Moreover, corporal punishment was administered (with straps or, better, switches) only if the patient was conscious of his misdeed and his punishment or could be induced through no other, milder means to obey the attendant. The report also mentions many other forbidden punitive devices: a trough in which patients

Wilhelm Wundt

could be confined; iron splints, manacles and fetters: chaining patients to the floor or to posts, flogging them, dipping them in water, or brandishing red-hot irons. Under certain conditions, however, attendants had recouse to cloth trusses, sacks, Autenrieth's mask and Cox's swing.

This brings us to a number of discoveries which were supposed to serve ingenious ends in specific instances and which for several decades had a pronounced influence on the treatment of the insane. Stress was placed on repressing the symptoms of mental illness, directing attention along the appropriate channel, promoting healthy thinking, stimulating the emotions and training the will. Restraining devices were now used to repress symptoms associated with particular mental conditions just as they had once been used for security reasons. Their number was augmented by a series of newer developments. Typical are the swaddling basket which Heinroth recommended especially for women, the coffin and the English booth or clockcase in which the recalcitrant or delirious patient was imprisoned with only his face exposed. The latter was to be used, according to Nostiz, only in rare cases in which the restless behavior of the patient stemmed from a bad will or from open defiance rather than from his illness. Schneider added to his description a characteristic statement: "We must at the same time do everything possible to prevent the patient from opening it, for if he should, his rage would know no bounds."

The same purpose was served by Horn's invention—a long, wide bag reinforced with oilcloth. The bag was pulled over the patient's head and tied beneath his feet. "It restrains the patient," explained Horn. "It shocks him by making him aware of his confinement and causes him to suspect or realize the fruitlessness of any attempt to stir up troubles." He also claimed that many restless, troublesome lunatics—even after other measures had failed to make them obedient, orderly and calm—responded to it by developing a more serene state of mind, by becoming more tractable, and by becoming more responsive to other, indirect psychic treatments. Many patients who refused to eat were so impressed by the threat of the bag "that they took a new lease on life and began once more to enjoy the food which they had stubbornly refused." One patient unfortunately died as a result of this treatment, and Horn thought it advisable to discard it. The same doctor named as one of the most innocuous, comfortable and safest device for calming patients the cruciform stance. The patient was harnessed and tied in a standing position, and with arms outstretched for 8 or 10 hours. This was supposed to mitigate delirious outbursts, encourage fatigue and sleep, render the patient harmless and obedient, and awaken in him a feeling of respect for the doctor. After it had been used a number of times, lunatics were often so frightened that the mere sight of it immediately made them orderly and obedient. For this reason it was particularly appropriate for punishing those who might injure others through misuse of their hands or feet, or who might adversely affect discipline within the institution through their obstinacy or their belligerent, recalcitrant, and uncooperative behavior. Neumann recommended it as "the best possible punishment for the worst transgressions of the insane."

Other examples of restraining devices are Autenrieth's masks and bulbs. The first of these, fashioned from leather, kept the patient's mouth closed; his arms, of course, had to be secured at the same time. Its purpose was "to prevent senseless shouting or exessively loud howling and shrieking for no reason, and to eliminate complaints on the part of patients disturbed by the commotion. The wearing of this comic device thwarts the patient's will and often makes it easier for him to endure his troubles. The insane behave in many instances like mischievous, undisciplined children who shout, cry and rant to give vent to their displeasure and naughtiness, and who become all the more vociferous when reprimanded.... But when they are forced to wear this contrivance, they are deprived of the one weapon with which they can avenge themselves and gradually made conscious of their total impotence." Less effective was the bulb-shaped gag carved from hard wood and secured inside the patient's mouth to impede his speech, though not his bellowing. Wire masks prevented spitting and biting.

A second group of devices for handling mental patients derived from an idea advanced by Erasmus Darwin and perfected by Cox—revolving machines. In these the patient was either turned on his own axis while seated in a chair or tied to a bed with his head pointed outward and describing a circle. The patient was given from 40 to 60 turns per minute. The effects, especially those produced by the revolving bed, were extraordinary. Centrifugal force drove the blood to the brain, and this caused intense anxiety, false sensations, fear of suffocation, nausea, vertigo, vomiting, urination and defecation, and finally bleeding under the conjunctiva tunica. Healthy persons usually begged for the machine to be stopped before two minutes had passed, yet many mental patients endured the experience for as long as 4 minutes. This contrivance was used for delirious, melancholic, obstinate, and uncooperative mental patients to train them to submit to discipline, to live according to prescribed regulations, and above all, to be obedient. It was also used for patients with suicidal tendencies, for those who refuse to eat, for silent, passive, unco-operative patients, for epileptics and for "general madness." "If this does not help," said Heinroth, "nothing will."

Both the revolving chair and Hallaran's swing, constructed on the same principle, produced similar, though weaker, effects. The former could be rotated so fast "that a healthy, rational man would lose everything in his stomach in five minutes." It therefore functioned well as an inexpensive emetic. Knight recommended it for constipation and for dyspepsia or hyperacidity. Through the "happy union" of vertigo and vomiting "strong convulsions can be induced throughout the organism, and these often have a most salubrious effect." Enraged patients, Horn wrote, became calm and agitated, restless patients became obedient and orderly; lazy, sluggish patients became alert and industrious. These effects could also be intensified and augmented by fear; for instance, the revolving chair could be placed in a dark, musty room where there were unusual noises, penetrating scents, or other strong stimuli. Cox was of the opinion that voyages at sea would serve the same purpose. He and several other doctors looked upon the revolving chair as an excellent remedy even in the most hopeless cases. "The patient's sensitivity, his slowness in becoming adjusted to the such devices, the degree to which he is affected by them and his antipathy toward them," explained Horn, "will determine the effectiveness of the treatment." Other harmless contrivances were the restraining cradle in which the patient might be imprisoned for hours and rocked back and forth (in the manner recommended by Celsus to combat sleeplessness) and suspended mats inside which the patient was pulled up and down or swung back and forth. He could be dropped suddenly into water or sprayed with a jet. The tense expectation of the unpleasant event was supposed to be effective in the treatment of vertigo. Chiarugi's unnamed translator mentioned an "extremely energetic lunatic" who became calm after he had been bound with a rope and left hanging for a few hours.

Another principle underlay the "hollow wheel" suggested by Reil and constructed by Hayner. Here the aim was to divert the patient from his aberrant course, to lead him back from the world of his dreams to the world of reality. It was to block the stream of erratic, fragmentary thoughts, direct his attention toward the attainment of a definite goal and to awaken and identify his self-consciousness. To accomplish these aims Hayner built a huge padded wheel, designed in much the same way as a treadmill, in which the patient was imprisoned. Unless he remained completely motionless, the patient had to run either forward or backward, and the decision to rest or to move about was his alone. Any attempt to damage the wheel could easily be prevented by a shove to set the patient in motion. Thus he could, if freed at times to satisfy his physical needs, spend from 36 to 48 hours in the wheel and would then be "either tractable and obedient as a result of the settling effect of the wheel" or so fatigued by the constant pace that he would easily fall asleep, his mind relaxed and the paroxysm mitigated. The device had a remarkably beneficial effect on a patient in Sonnenstein, Nostiz reported; it marked the first step in the return of self-consciousness. Later, however, Hayner himself renounced its use.

Alienists of that era did not give their unanimous endorsement to such contrivances. Damerow, for instance, wrote in 1829: "These mechanical devices are not without interest historically, but instruments that will be effective in the treatment of insanity are yet to be perfected. Even those who advocate them seem indifferent with respect to their application. We can be certain that they will later be replaced by better, more ingenious devices; perhaps after a few centuries they will be relegated to museums and exhibited to admiring visitors as curiosities." His prediction was soon fulfilled.

Occasionally we also find statements which anticipate by far certain stages in the development of psychaitry. Chiarugi, who considered lashings proper "in the case of many unruly, delirious patients," declared such punishment improper, harmful, cruel and inhumane when patients were irrational and unresponsive to fear, dangerous when they were rabid, and fatal under other circumstances. He added that since beatings had been forbidden in the Florentine hospital, delirious patients had been recovering more often than formerly. The practice of using threats and lashes to correct the thinking of the insane was ineffective in that it merely excited them and fortified their obstinacy; it was easier to lead them back to the world of reality through indirect means and gradually to influence their thinking. One should pamper them, consent to whatever might calm them, and laugh at them.

"A wise and enlightened man," said Pinel, "sees in the outbursts of the insane nothing more than an automatic inpulse or rather a necessary discharge of nervous energy; it should cause no more annoyance than the impact of a stone that falls because of its own weight. He will permit such madmen to have full freedom of movement so long as their safety or the safety of others is not imperiled and will cleverly hide from them the restraining devices to be used, just as if they had to obey only the laws of necessity.... It should be an ironclad rule in every hospital that the insane be allowed every freedom consonant with good sense; that the degree of coercion be determined by the severity of the outburst; that mistreatment and violence on the part of hospital workers be prohibited; that duties be carried out at the proper time with indulgence and firmness."

Knight recommended that unhealthy ideas be disregarded and an attempt made to focus attention on neutral subjects. "In treating the insane," he wrote, "one should use sympathy and forebearance. Sometimes arrogance and even gross insults are not merely to be tolerated but even borne cheerfully if the patient is unaware of the nature of the insult. Here psychiatric treatment rules out even the slightest degree of coercion." Against punishment Hayner had this to say: "Hallucinations or delusions are almost always responsible for outrages on the part of patients. Unpleasant mental impressions can effectively curtail abnormal psychic conflicts, but corrective measures should never appear to be wholly punitive since punishment would be effective only if the patient were capable of exercising his will. Since he is irrational and cannot punishment seems to him unjust." Less logically, Roller explained in 1831 that a mental patient ought occasionally to feel that whatever had been done to him was intended as punishment even though this had not been the case. He believed in the observance of quasi-judicial proceedings and in swift, inexorable punishment, but warned against the use of punitive measures resembling those ordinarily decreed by courts since the ideas evoked them could only aggravate the patient's condition. Noteworthy is Amelung's conviction that the insane were not to be treated like young children but like adults, and that odd, childish, ridiculous regulations were to be avoided since they either remained ineffective or generated indignation and mistrust. "Without question the best results have been achieved by doctors who appear to be friendly and trustworthy, who conduct themselves affably and (depending on the character of the patient) even jocularly, and who remain calm in the face of the most violent, annoying, and unpleasant outburst on the part of the deranged or emotionally disturbed inmate—and who nevertheless exhibit seriousness and strictness in dealing with the disorderly, obstinate, or malicious patient who retains some degree of rationality."

We find similar expressions in the writing of Hayner and Leupoldt. The former insisted that the patient be allowed freedom "to the extent that it does not endanger the life of the patient or the lives of his fellow sufferers, and so long as it does not interfere with institutional discipline.... Insofar as possible, patients should be treated with mildness and forebearance, and as if they were rational." Against this, Leupoldt stated bluntly: "The insane are generally credited with being more rational than they often are; our success in treating them will be enhanced by a knowledge of the facts."

Reil tried logically to elaborate a psychiatric treatment of the insane. Though he lacked sufficient experience, he managed to adumbrate specific principles. He reasoned, obviously on the basis of Pinel's views, that the patient had first to be made obedient so that he could be influenced by the doctor. "Through strong, painful impressions we capture the patient's attention, accustom him to unconditional obedience, and indelibly imprint in his heart the

The fractious patient in spread eagle form receiving medical treatment of' Douch bath in the Penn. Hospital for the Insane, July 4th, 1868.
E. Haskell.

feeling of necessity. The will of his superior must be such a firm, immutable law for him that he will no more resist it that he would rebel against the elements." To achieve this, the doctor was always supposed to make allowances for the needs of a particular patient. In the beginning, however, some measure of sternness was always required. To subjugate the patient, the doctor had first to deprive him of every prop and make him feel absolutely helpless. That is why he had to be taken from his home and his accustomed surroundings and brought under lugubrious and frightful circumstances (when possible, by night and through detours) to a strange asylum. "As he approaches he hears drumbeats and cannon shots; he crosses a series of bridges and is received by a darkskinned man.... The officials speak a strange, sonorous language.... An entrance under such ominous circumstances can counteract forthwith any desire to disobey." Short commands, which were immediately and unhesitatingly obeyed, then broke down all resistance.

Once resistance had been broken, coercion ceased and the doctor adopted the opposite pattern of behavior. He dealt with the patient openly and in a friendly manner. giving him things that were pleasing to him for his good conduct. An attempt was made to accustom him to orderliness and conformity, to awaken his attention, and finally to require him to engage in specific activities. Impressions that excited pleasure or disgust accomplished the first aim, as did strong stimuli of all kinds, intriguing and impressive objects, and unusual experiences. "For instance, the patient is brought into a pitch-black, deathly-quiet cellar filled with the most bizarre, moving and motionless, dead and living objects. Among the objects used to produce a gruesome impression might be balloons, sinks, icicles, men dressed in furs, marble statues, and eerie, unseen hands that stroke the patient's beard." Other possibilities included snake-bites, pistol shots, cannon shots, the piercing sound of a wind instrument, the sustained vibrations of a 32-foot pipe organ, punctuated beats on a Turkish drum, a savage cacophony in which were mingled the noise of drums, bells, shawms, human voices, the howling of animals, pianos and sundry musical renditions. Theatrical performances involving executioners and dead people who had returned from the grave were supposed to be effective. Here "Don Quixote was dubbed a knight, fictitious babies were delivered, lunatics were trepanned, contrite sinners were ceremoniously absolved of their sins."

Such strong mental impressions and such vivid appeals to the imagination were supposed to awaken the patient from his befuddled state. "Use a set of pulleys to elevate him to the top of a huge vault so that he dangles like Absalon between heaven and earth, discharge a cannon, don a frightening disguise and brandish a red-hot iron as you approach him, throw him into a raging stream, pretend to offer him to wild animals, abandon him to the raillery of bugbears and demons or let him sail through the air on a fire-breathing dragon. An underground vault can suddenly be transformed from Hell with all its terrors to a magic temple in which ceremonial music is played while beautiful scenes are evoked out of nothingness by the magic power of a charming nymph."

To force the patient to engage in some constructive activity, Reil suggested that he be confronted with a pretended danger. This would force him to discover the instrument of his own salvation and to put it to use. He was led into a special garden. There as he walked through hedges and blind passageways he was sprayed and drenched with water. As he approached an inviting resting spot he was met by a ferocious beast; in another spot he sank into the ground or fell into a grave from which he could emerge only after an unrelenting struggle. If he was lazy he had to pump water from a pit until it reached the level of his throat, walk through narrow winding paths, swim, paddle a small skiff and ride a frightful, unruly horse.

He was supposed also to work, at first with his hands and with equipment, but later to perform more complex tasks. Reil recommended basket-weaving, landscaping, dancing, balancing, calesthenics, vaulting, horseshoes, knitting, painting, sketching, singing, music and play-acting. He urged that patients write, solve problems, correct proofs and keep diaries. He also recommended that patients be allowed to engage in construction work and that the planning and supervision be carried out by the brighter ones. Prompt execution of orders given by superiors was essential. Patients were allowed to perform diverse mental tasks, their emotional life was carefully controlled, and their minds were trained through all sorts of tests "Thus through psychic stimuli we lead the patient from the depths of utter senselessness to complete rationality."

Every experienced alienist soon recognized the worth of meaningful activity, especially farming and gardening, in the treatment of mental patients. The story of the Scottish farmer who achieved good results by hitching patients to the plow or harrow like draft animals, first related by Gregory in his lectures, has been retold countless times. We find repeated references to the Saragossa institution with the inscription *"urbis et orbis."* Pinel reported that patients evidenced improvement after they had been persuaded to engage in agricultural pursuits. "Experience repeatedly shows," he added, "that this is the surest and most effective means of helping the patient to regain his sanity, and that the nobleman who arrogantly rejects any thought of manual labor has the privilege of perpetuating his senseless aberration and his delirium."

Rush cited a number of cases in which patients recovered after they had again taken up their favorite pursuits. He recommended that patients be allowed to read books aloud, memorize and write. Esquirol, Heinroth, Langermann, Willis, Jacobi and many others extolled the efficacy of work, through both the activity itself and the feeling of satisfaction that resulted from the activity. Horn attached little importance to the latter consideration. He urged only that the work be performed correctly and punctually under strict supervision; indeed, he even maintained that all labor should be forced labor since results were generally better when it was performed under duress. "Satisfaction and delight are beneficial much less frequently than punishment and invective." These views, prompted mainly perhaps by the dire conditions which prevailed in Charité and which he vividly described, led him to prescribe aimless tasks for patients to perform—digging and refilling trenches, pulling light coaches back and forth or drilling with wooden weapons under the leadership of non-commissioned officers. The last activity was also introduced at Sonnenstein.

Leupoldt reasoned on the contrary that work should not be performed too mechanically, that intervening conversations should focus attention on the nature and purpose of the work at hand and on the reasons for adopting particular measures. "This involves the use of reason and gradually encourages the use of the patient's full faculties; it banishes stupidity, rules out capriciousness, dissipates delusions, hallucinations, and idle speculation, accustoms the patient to dealing with material objects and the world of reality." The same opinion was voiced by Jacobi and Neumann, who pointed out that inane tasks angered and irritated patients and made them feel as if they were pawns to be used for the doctor's amusement. "They study and hate and execute their tasks reluctantly," Neumann added. "Yes, they learn to hate us because we instill in them the notion that they alone are rational while we are irrational—a notion frequently acquired by the insane."

Travel was often recommended for diversion, both at the onset of mental illness and during recuperation. It was hoped that travel would curtail and repress morbific ideas and that it would fortify the will by exposing the patient to strange surroundings. Heinroth maintained, in contrast to present-day thinking, that "interesting travels involving varied attractions, hardships, and activities" were effective in treating melancholia. "Travel is a universal medicine for such patients," he said. "This is also the best way for the patient to regain a lost appetite or recover from loss of sleep, to banish shyness, fear and gloom, to prepare to return to the life and occupation from which he has fled."

Music and singing were extolled by Haindorf and Schneider. Religious instruction and spiritual counseling were also stressed, for instance, by Jacobi, Roller, Zeller and especially Heinroth. "When we become better acquainted with it," wrote the latter, "we realize that religion and religion alone can effectively ward off every possible type of mental illness."

The broad outlines of the practice of psychiatry as it existed a century ago have been revealed by our cursory survey: negligent and brutal treatment of the insane; improper living conditions and inadequate medical care; beclouded and false notions concerning the nature and cause of insanity; senseless, haphazard, and at times harmful therapeutic measures which aggravated the plight of those afflicted by mental illness. It would be wrong to assume that such practices precluded the existence of others which are sanctioned today. Long before that time there were isolated instances in which mental patients were cared for systematically and sympathetically. There were also a number of doctors whose rich experience or genius afforded a better understanding of mental diseases and who developed sound methods of treatment because they viewed patients sympathetically and without prejudice. Alone these exceptional men could neither modify existing practices nor improve the lot of the masses; they were the seeds from which under more propitious conditions would spring the modern science of psychiatry.

A decisive step in the right direction was the construction of asylums and, along with this, the development of the psychiatric profession. Though hospitals for the insane were not unknown during the eighteenth century, it was not until the first decade of the next century that separate mental institutions were erected in great numbers. Statistics compiled by Lahr reveal that in Germany such institutions had been erected before 1800 in Rockwinkel, Frankfurt, Neuss, Blankenburg, Waldheim, Lübeck and Bayreuth. The oldest one in France was in Avignon (1681); in England, Springfield (1741); in Italy, Florence (1645); in Poland, Warsaw (1728); in Austria, Salzburg

(1772); in Denmark. Copenhagen (1766); and in Sweden, Upsala (1766). But these institutions were nothing more than dumping grounds for raging, incurable derelicts; there was small hope that any of their inmates would ever recover. Autenrieth observed as late as 1807 that only incurable patients were taken to the public asylums "where no one tries to effect cures," while others had to be taken to private doctors who might undertake to cure them either through compassion or through ambition. He added that doctors were easily discouraged "by the prospect of having to engage in activities of this kind for an inordinate period of time."

Haindorf explained in 1811 that under the conditions which then prevailed in public asylums in Germany, "only a few can be cured by science unless fate works miracles." As late as 1821 Vering sanctioned dispatching a mental patient to an asylum in spite of the dire consequences entailed by uprooting him from his accustomed surroundings and thrusting him into a strange situation, especially if he found himself imprisoned and at the mercy of a strange warden in an institution which seemed more like a jail than a hospital. This might not have harmed imbeciles, maniacs and lunatics; it might even have proved to be beneficial under certain circumstances. On other patients, however, it made a painful, indelible impression, and one that was daily revived by the sight of unfortunate comrades—pitiable, senseless creatures who raged and screamed and endured heart-rending misery. Such considerations still prevent patients from being placed in institutions under a wholly different set of circumstances, until they become, in lay terms, "ripe." Vering recommended that an attempt first be made to provide competent care in the home and that the patient be placed in

Benjamin Rush

an institution only if he had failed to show improvement over a six-month period. Nostiz and others voiced the charge, still heard today, that patients were unjustly deprived of their freedom. "We have ample proof," declared Hock, "that certain scoundrels, through greed or maliciousness, have kept rational people locked in the asylum."

For all that, humane doctors and judicious administrators were constantly seeking to better the desperate situation of the mentally ill. Diverse plans were laid out for the construction of asylums; because of the aura of uncertainty surrounding the nature and treatment of mental diseases, however, and because of insufficient experience, these plans were often quixotic. Quite typical was the construction of a great number of tiny rooms, for it was assumed that each patient ought to have a cell to himself. In England asylums were modeled on prisons. Adjacent cell doors fronted on long corridors which could be guarded from a single vantage point. Designs were generally cruciform, circular, or radiate, as in the case of the Narrenturm opened in Vienna in 1784.

Anything that could have a beneficial influence on patients was also considered. "The asylum must be favorably situated," explained Reil. "It must be near lakes, streams, waterfalls, mountains and fields, cities and villages. It must provide facilities for farming, raising livestock and gardening." In that way patients could be distracted and kept busy in the manner dictated by their illness. There they can share in the diversions afforded by pastoral calm and urban delights or engage as circumstances require in gardening and agriculture or in professional and artistic activities in the city." He recommended that asylums be constructed like farmhouses and provided with gutters, showers and douches as well as with cellars, grottos, magic temples, a place for drill and calisthenics, facilities for concerts, plays and other intellectual activities, and finally, devices for frightening the patient and arousing the instinct for self-preservation. Frank recommended placing song-birds and exotic plants in the corridors and Aeolian harps in the windows. He also recommended that patients be given the opportunity to practice horsemanship, play at ninepins and ride the merry-go-round. Riding the merry-go-round was thought to be especially beneficial. The magic room was to be equipped with a trapdoor to enable patients to be dropped into the subterranean chamber and put to tests much like those administered by freemasons. Heinroth designed a simpler structure to serve as an educational institution. He also recommended friendly surroundings, pleasant strolls, gardens, fields, workshops, a functional library, physical apparatuses, a museum of natural history, facilities for practicing music, drawing and painting, toys, bowling-alleys and billiard tables. He urged that the staff include specialists in crafts, arts and sciences who could supervise or teach music, vocational training, natural history, physics, gymnastics, tailoring, shoe-making and carpentry.

Because of their lack of precision, novelty and high cost, such plans could never be put into practice. It was possible occasionally to arrange mediocre accomodations for a rather large number of mental patients in old castles, cloisters and hospitals and to provide them with specialized treatment and care. Methodical study of the needs of patients pointed up the urgency of constructing special institutions for curable patients whose suffering was thought to be so intensified by their association with the others as to make them also incurable. "Incurable patients will impress them in such a way as to prevent recovery," said Reil. "They will cause relapses and thwart the best-laid plans for effecting a cure. The two groups must not be allowed to have the slightest contact with each other." Horn also reasoned that unavoidable contact and agitation entailed by a return of paroxysms had a prejudicial effect on the patient on the road to recovery.

Such considerations led to the construction of additional facilities for caring for the insane in Sonnenstein (1811), Sieburg (1815) and, later, of completely new structures for these purposes in Sachsenberg (1830). These trailblazing accomplishments had far-reaching results. "Sonnenstein was the dawn of a new day in the treatment of mental disease in Germany," wrote Damerow. "The bright rays from this height brought light, warmth and life into other institutions where darkness prevailed; there arose the persistent hope, the precarious belief that complete recovery from mental disease was not simply a random phenomenon, and the ripened fruit of knowledge spread far and wide throughout the world of the insane seeds of humanity and science which took root and yielded an abundant harvest." From all quarters came visitors to study the new institutions, draw inspiration from them, and plan similar structures.

We can best assess the effect of the rapid spread of well-operated institutions on the lay public by recalling how patients had formerly been treated. In 1845 Pitsch reported that in Pomerania, where the Rugenwalde institution was opened in 1841, many mental patients were cared for and supervised by distant relatives and selfish individuals who because they were underpaid, "frequently treated the half-naked lunatics who wandered through towns and villages molesting the public worse than animals, and allowed them to search in neighboring houses for crusts of bread to satisfy their hunger, bedded them down for the night on straw-covered floors of wretched stalls, abandoned them for the most part to their sad fate, chastized them and used chains or ropes to restrain their delirious paroxysms (the pitiful bodies of patients admitted to the institution are still scarred), and allowed them to be brutalized by filth and vermin. This description is shocking but not exaggerated; the sordid facts make changes imperative... Most of the patients admitted to date to the institution have arrived in a wretched condition. Ill-clad and ill-nourished, dirty and beastly, they could no longer be entrusted to private individuals for care; they had nothing in common with other men except their shape." Dahl related in a report for the year 1859 that in many places in Norway mental patients were turned over to individual proprietors, put on the block at a public auction, and sold to the highest bidder.

One great short-coming was the fact that admission to an institution was frequently delayed by routine formalities as well as by overcrowded conditions that soon began to prevail, with the result that long waiting lists accrued. Jacobi reckoned that a patient could be admitted under favorable circumstances in two or at most ten days while the normal process required about three weeks. There is evidence to show however, that years sometimes passed before the papers required for admission to the Sonnenstein institution could be completed. The dangers and actual harm entailed by such delays need not be elaborated. Today, especially in large cities, almost every critical case can be given prompt attention.

It has by no means been easy to retrace the steps

through which our institutions have passed. What today seems apparent and logical—prompt, competent attention to the needs of every mental patient, treatment and care utilizing all the tools made available by knowledge and experience—at first met with general opposition. What is new and unfamiliar is often resisted. By dint of much hard work, tenacity, personal sacrifice and unflagging enthusiasm, our predecessors generally managed to overcome difficulties posed by the nature of mental illness and, more important still, by misunderstanding and apathy on the part of the masses as well as by the scarcity of therapeutic devices or measures at their disposal. The vast amount of work expended in this area during the course of the century is suggested by the existence in Germany in 1911 of 187 public asylums for the insane, 16 university clinics, 5 mental wards in military hospitals, 11 wards in penal institutions, 225 private institutions, and 85 institutions for alcoholics, patients suffering from nervous disorders and degenerates. Mental patients and imbeciles admitted to these institutions numbered 143,410. Such results could not have been achieved, of course, without the energetic cooperation of competent officers and administrators. After doctors succeeded in focusing their attention on the necessity of providing for the insane, they vied with each other in perfecting ideal arrangements. Hardenberg, Nostiz and Jankendorf merit special mention, for they were among the first to appreciate fully the problems posed by insanity and to spare nothing in an attempt to solve them.

Every newly established institution for the insane provided a vast, ever-expanding reservoir or experience. Thus there gradually evolved a group of trained observers, a psychiatric profession whose main concern was the study of psychic symptoms and the discovery of means for curing mental disease. In 1911 there were already 1376 practicing alienists in Germany. The first call to join ranks had already been issued in 1827 by Ennemoser and Ruer; the present-day German psychiatric association traces its origin back to 1842; formalized in 1860 and 1864, it today numbers 700 members.

On the basis of practical experience thus acquired, the physician was soon assigned the most important role in German institutions (first, apparently, by Sieburg). Administrative details were under his control, though Reil still advocated a triumvirate composed of the superintendent, physician, and psychologist and subject to no higher authority. "If therapy of any kind is to be effective in an institution for the insane," explained Haindorf, "everything except finance must be under the direction of a doctor trained in psychology." Heinroth stated emphatically: "The doctor is the soul of the institution, and the whole operation must be carried out according to his insights and purposes." He sketched this portrait of the doctor: "It is not absolutely necessary for him to possess an imposing physique, voice or glance; it is to his advantage, however, if he does. In any event he must possess good health and physical endurance if, for instance, he is to withstand the stress of being awakened at night. He must be fearless and must not shun toil; he must not be hot-headed and violent or in the slightest degree lazy and listless. His profession must interest him and take first place in his life; he must practice it with fervor and with love. He must be sincere, trustworthy and sympathetic, not stubborn and transigent, rude and harsh, and surely not fulsome and effeminate. He must have the power to be firm as well as gentle since circumstances may dictate either firmness or gentleness. He must be not only a man of science and art but also a doctor in the broad sense of the word—one educated through study and skilled through practice. He must be neither a rank empiricist nor an idle speculator. He must adhere to the world of nature and live in the world of ideas. He must be guided by reason in his struggle against the absence of reason. He must be experienced in the ways of the world and know how to treat men as individuals. Finally, he must thoroughly understand from both the theoretical and the practical viewpoint the psychic methods of treatment of every expert, not just one therapeutic practice. He must have the capacity to experiment and to observe. If he is to advance the science of psychiatry, he must exhibit intelligence, not fanaticism; true genius is methodical but not mechanical."

Haindorf was equally exacting. He required of his "doctors for the insane" perfect humanity, education of the mind and heart through science, art and experience in the ways of the world, and decisive speech and conduct together with pleasing, dignified external features. "Along with the gentle character of a woman he must have the harshness and strength of a man; in his conduct he must blend friendship, love and kindliness in just proportion with aloofness, harshness and strictness and always know how through his humane comportment to win the trust of his patients." Leupoldt expressed himself more forcefully: "An alienist must be, or rather must have been, a Faust. He must have had intimate contact with the good and the bad and must possess a vast store of psychic experiences; he must be no stranger to mire and scum found at the lowest level of human existence nor to the lofty heights attained by genius; he must have had some personal contact with false, dark mysticism as well as with its counterpart which is studied but unfounded presumptuousness; he must have experienced both emotional turmoil and biting scepticism; knowing the idolatry of senseless surrender to the pleasures of the mind and of somber, painful withdrawal from the world, he must strike a balance between inconstancy and conformity—and be a skilled, many-sided, whole, rational man and at the same time a competent doctor."

Oegg sketched a similar portrait: "The doctor who treats the insane must be talented and predisposed to working with such patients. These qualities must be innate; they cannot be cultivated. He must know the essentials of philosophy, psychology and medicine; furthermore, he must be able to understand men and get along well with them. He must be fearless, self-possessed, alert and able to grasp facts readily. Above all, in each instance he must be able to make decisions that will be appropriate to a particular situation and to a particular plan of treatment. He must have patience and tolerance to enable him to endure calmly unpleasant situations. He must blend kindness and sympathy with strictness and, where necessary, with studied harshness in order to avoid showing either too little or too much concern and thereby destroying the respect and reverence which is his due. His love for science must inspire indefatigable activity and profound concern over the patient's condition. He must have a flawless character, integrity, and self-control that will enable him to resist becoming involved in schemes through which he might safely and easily acquire wealth illegally. He should stand as a shining example through his noble self-sacrifice for the benefit of patients."

Men were found who could meet such rigid require-

Fool's Tower in Vienna

ments and who could also transform the existing institutions for the insane and gradually adapt them to the needs of psychiatry. Today we can note with pride that the elaboration of facilities for the treatment of the insane was effected through the efforts of a great number of outstanding personalities—distinguished physicians, brilliant researchers, far-sighted and strong-willed administrators and selfless humanitarians. This is probably due to the fact that the virgin territory of psychiatry attracted only men who possessed outstanding qualifications for the task at hand.

The first fruit of this new development was the victory of scientific observation over philosophical and moral meditation. The pattern followed by mental diseases, their intimate relation to physical injuries, and their role in the debasement and destruction of the personality could not escape men who were in close contact daily with patients. At the same time researchers stressed the value of individual findings, and these are the heart of the scientific method. Even though in the long run the teachings of the somatic school proved to be less important than Jacobi had thought, new support was provided for the conviction, advanced earlier by countless researchers, that insanity was due to a malfunctioning of the brain, brought on either by a defective anlage or other causes. The medical theory of mental illness is still upheld by such men as Griesinger, who by virtue of his eminent role in the reform of clinical medicine was especially qualified to forge a closer link between psychiatry, which had been allowed to develop independently in institutions for the insane, and its sister sciences. Griesinger stressed the fact that mental diseases comprised only one group of brain disorders and could be understood only in this context. A series of psychic symptoms seemed to him to offer a basis for comparison with certain diseases of the brain and spinal cord; for example, he likened moria and paralysis agitans, mania and epilepsy, imbecility and paralysis. He demanded a closer scientific alliance of psychiatry and neurology—something which could be achieved at first only in universities. Meynert and Wernicke followed a similar course in that they sought to arrive at an understanding of mental illness by studying the structure of the brain and to put to use in psychiatry the results of experiments involving patients with brain diseases.

The establishment of institutions for the insane also made it possible to train young doctors in psychiatry. Schools could be set up and the findings of individual researchers disseminated. Chiarugi in Florence was apparently the first to give instruction in psychiatry; he was followed by Pinel (1814) and by Esquirol (1817), whose classes were regularly attended by many students. The first German professors of psychiatry were Horn, who apparently initiated his clinical studies in Berlin in 1806, and Heinroth, who began his work in Leipzig in 1811. Nostiz complained that a chair of music was considered indispensable long before the first chair of psychiatry was ever established. In Bavaria psychiatric instruction dates back to 1833, when Marcus gave the first lectures in the Juliusspital in Wurzburg. Next came Solbrig in Erlangen (1849) and in Munich (1861). For several decades, however, instruction in psychiatry was offered in hospital wards and asylums located near universities. Though Leupoldt in 1828 had expressed the hope that an independent psychiatric clinic could soon be established, the first such German clinic was not built until 1878. This one, in Heidelberg, was the first in a long series. Today German medical schools have regular chairs for psychiatry and exemplary instructional facilities. We are in this respect superior to all other nations of the world.

This development unfortunately loosened the link between clinics and institutions for the insane. Clinics, which often gave free reign to those interested in neurology, failed by far with respect to both their aims and their procedures to meet the needs of institutional psychiatry; psychiatric institutions, because of their isolation, the restricted nature of their mission and various other unfavorable circumstances, risked losing contact with the very heart of science. In the future one of the most important tasks for both types of researchers will be to protect our emerging science against the dangers inherent in such alienation. Not until 1904, long after they had been introduced in Bavaria (1861), were examinations first administered to doctors who intended to practice psychiatry.

An imposing body of knowledge and a desire to share it with others were responsible for the creation of a vast quantity of technical literature, the compilation of textbooks, and the founding of periodicals. The first German textbooks were those by Haindorf (1811) and by Vering (1817). These were soon supplemented by a long series of others—by Heinroth, Neumann, Jacobi, Ideler, Friedrich, Blumröder, Bird, Kieser, Flemming, and Griesinger, who has already contributed more than thirty volumes toward the advancement of our science. The first psychiatric journals, founded by Heil between 1805 and 1808, were edited by philosophers and psychologists.

In his journal for doctors whose field of specialization was the mind, Mass came closer to a sound medical position but left ample room for unscientific views. The

Allgemeine Zeitschrift für Psychiatrie has been published continuously since 1844. Today in Germany alone we have at our disposal more than a dozen journals devoted to the field of psychiatry in general or to separate psychiatric disciplines.

The next task of the emerging science was the description and delineation of different types of mental illness. A giant stride in this direction was the publication in 1844 of Jacob's work on delirium, intended as the first part of an exhaustive account based on long and patient observation of patients, of the different forms of insanity. Although Esquirol had already followed a similar plan, the German work excelled all previous undertakings in scope, depth and detail. It can serve as a model for researchers now clamoring in increasing numbers to advance science by studying and describing exactly and in detail circumscribed areas of experience. French clinicians can boast brilliant accomplishments in this direction; the long and unbroken tradition of the Parisian school, unparalled opportunities for observation in the metropolis, good logic, and unparalleled talent for observing and reporting facts contributed to their success. They did much to advance our knowledge of paralysis, cyclic psychosis, mental disorders following acute illnesses, hysteria, paranoia, and different forms of degenerative insanity.

Progress was slower in Germany. Here researchers had been impressed by a fact noted earlier by Chiarugi and Esquirol: the same distance was known to assume strikingly different forms during its course. For instance, French alienists had shown that this was true of cyclic delirium. On this fact Guislain based his notion that diverse clinical pictures were outward expressions of an inner struggle to compensate for psychic traumas. That explained the initial onset of the feeling of sadness or melancholia as a direct result of a stimulus, the subsequent onset of anger and mania as a result of the reaction triggered by the instinct for self-preservation. Other forms of compensation included irresoluteness or caprice as a manifestation of folly, nervous tension in the form of ecstasy, convulsions and finally, false notions in the form of either megalomania or delusions of persecution. That different symptoms corresponded to differences in personality and anlage was a view advanced by Jacobi in his description of temperaments.

Guislain's idea, later expounded by Zeller, adopted by Hagen and integrated by Griesinger into his exposition of psychiatry, apparently supported the view that different phases in the progress of insanity were generally marked by distinct clinical symptoms and associated with strong emotional agitation; delirium and delusion were thought to be mild and curable stages of the disease while the more pronounced disorders of the mind and will, such as lunacy and imbecility, were thought to lead to incurable asthenia. Since there were no sharp lines of distinction between the different types of insanity, classification of individual cases was highly arbitrary. Attempts to settle the issue of classification met with failure. Gudden considered the task of identifying and classifying the different types of mental disease insoluble and rejected every attempt to induce him to express an opinion on the issue by saying, "I don't know."

Snell and Westphal demonstrated that the Zeller-Griesinger theory was untenable by showing that lunacy was not always the terminal point of a mental disorder associated with emotional agitation but that it could develop independently and as a "primary" condition.

The situation was complicated unduly by the fact that attempts to classify individual cases were based almost invariably on the external symptoms of insanity; these fluctuating and interpenetrating symptoms simply could not be delineated and used as a basis for classification. Only gradually did there emerge from this confusion distinct classifications based on the mental condition of the patient and corresponding apparently to identical causal conditions: feverish delirium (its relation to mental illness had long been a controversial issue), alcoholic disorders, senility, congenital asthenia. Furthermore, the confused mass of clinical symptoms revealed the sharp outlines of progressive paralysis, identified earlier by French doctors, when Griesinger posited it as an occasional concomitant of insanity.

Progressive paralysis was characterized by symptoms associated with brain disease and by its fatal termination. Esquirol, who accurately described its symptoms, observed that halting speech portended death and produced evidence to show that the disease followed a regular course and at the same time involved specific changes in the brain. Kahlbaum seized upon this example in an attempt to clarify the classification of mental diseases. He was the first to stress the necessity of juxtaposing the condition of the patient, his transitory symptoms and the basic pattern underlying his disease. The condition of one and the the same patient may change often and in diverse ways, with the result that in the absence of other clues any attempt to rescue him from his plight is doomed to failure. Moreover, identical or remarkably similar symptoms can accompany wholly dissimilar diseases while their inner nature can be revealed only through their progress and termination and, in some instances, through an autopsy.

On the basis of such considerations Kahlbaum sought to delineate a second pattern of illness similar to that of paralysis and, like it, embracing both mental disorders and physical concomitants: catatonia, in which muscular tension provided a basis for comparison with paralysis. Although his interpretation is open to criticism, Kahlbaum deserves credit for having suggested the right approach. Careful attention to the progress and termination of mental disorders, information gleaned in some instances from autopsies, and insight into underlying causes have made possible the juxtaposition of a vast array of evidence and often diagnosis on the basis of symptom pattern. We can today formulate in specific terms what earlier doctors could surmise but not prove. The result is that a beginner is able in countless instances to predict the course of a disease, or at least its general pattern, more accurately than could the older alienist after ten years of experience. Although we are still unsure of all the answers, it seems that the right path has been discovered and that patient work will bring us ever nearer to our goal.

Along with our knowledge has come a lack of confidence in the efficacy of our medical practices. We know now that the fate of our patient is determined mainly by the development of the disease. We can often mitigate symptoms and establish conditions that will favor recovery, but we can rarely alter the course of the disease. Against this, our ability frequently to predict what will happen keeps us from falsely assuming, as did the older doctors, that our treatment will appreciably influence the outcome of the disease.

Gradually a foundation was laid for the scientific interpretation of observations made daily by the doctor. Exhaustive study showed that diverse sets of conditions alternated during the course of the same disease but always manifested an instrinsic homogeneity. Against this, certain sets of conditions, though characteristic of different disorders, at times resembled each other but were never wholly identical. Once the essential sameness of the diverse sets was understood and the distinction between sets characteristic of different disorders was refined through the retrospective study of their development, particular traits which had previously gone unnoticed appeared in the symptomology of each disorder.

The enlargement of our stock of research tools contributed significantly to the advancement of psychiatry. A thorough understanding of specific psychic conditions, achieved mainly through psychological research, makes it possible for us correctly to evaluate faint but significant variations in conduct even when we are unable to study in detail what goes on inside the patient. Moreover, we have at our disposal a number of diagnostic techniques utilizing secondary physical symptoms. We are able to diagnose with greater accuracy the physical condition of the mental patient because of everything learned from ancillary sciences dealing with diseases of the eyes, ears, heart and blood and from examining the pupils, reflexes, blood pressure, urine and feces, etc. Especially important in psychiatry is physical poise, which enabled Chiarugi and Esquirol to predict the termination of insanity and which has become an indispensable diagnostic tool. In some instances basal metabolism tests also yield valuable criteria; most significant, however, is the discovery of changes in the blood and spinal fluid caused by syphilis.

The conviction that the key to the understanding of

Adolph Meyer

insanity was to be found in the condition of the brain had already focused the attention of alienists on this organ. Neumann began his book on mental disease by presenting an outline of the anatomy of the brain; Haindorf concluded his treatise in the same way. Meckel tried to determine the specific gravity of brain tissue in the case of both sane and insane persons. When autopsies were performed, often the only observable changes related to plethora, bleeding, and constriction of the blood vessels. Often signs of increased or decreased flow of blood to the brain could be observed in patients. The theory that a blockage in the circulation of blood through the brain resulted in the appearance of diverse symptoms won numerous adherents, from Cox, Rush and Mayo in the old days to Wolff, who believed that he could base his prognosis on the mental patient's pulse, and to Meynert, who sought to explain the symptoms of melancholia and delirium by circulatory changes in distinct parts of the brain under the influence of vascular nerves. Charcteristic of the great significance attributed to such issues was Grashey's insistence, as a preliminary step toward research involving human beings, on conducting exhaustive experiments involving the circulation of water through elastic tubes.

Other researchers followed Griesinger's lead and concentrated on diseases of the brain and spinal column. Their problems were simpler, their findings more rewarding. Westphal, Hitzig, Fürstner, and above all Wernicke and his school (especially Liepmann) deserve praise for their accomplishments in this field; they provided psychiatry with a wealth of new data and knowledge, illuminating more than anything else diseases characterized by profound changes in the brain—paralysis, insanity caused by diseases of the brain or vascular system, and insanity caused by tumors.

The difficulty of their undertaking obliged the alienists to attempt in many instances, as the foregoing examples show, to try to reach their goal in a roundabout way, and they met with remarkable success when they ventured into contiguous territories. Their exhaustive studies relating to the anatomy of the brain are most impressive. Foremost were the contributions of Meynert and Gudden. Meynert provided us with an exact description of the structure of the brain and attempted to explain the interdependence of its separate divisions as well as their importance. Gudden studied its deterioration and formulated an ingenious system that enabled him slowly and painstakingly to expose the interdependence of nerve impulses and cell groups in the incredibly intricate structure. His students, especially Monakow and Nissl, followed in his footsteps while Wernicke and Obersteiner continued the work of Meynert. Obersteiner crowned his achievements by establishing in Vienna a great institution for brain research. At first discoveries relating to the anatomy of the brain unfortunately contributed less than might have been hoped to the science of psychiatry. Nevertheless, it was considered so important that chairs of psychiatry were occupied by men who had previously devoted all their attention to the physiology or the anatomy of the brain. This proves that psychiatry needed to be put on a firmer scientific basis; it also indicates that the importance of clinical practice was underrated.

A prime obstacle to understanding psychic processes was until recently the insurmountable difficulty of illuminating the delicate cerebral changes responsible for them. Post-mortem examinations contributed significantly to the advancement of the art of healing. The older doctors—Arnold, Esquirol, Guislain, and Greding, among others—were of course interested in performing autopsies to find the cause of diseases, but their efforts were for the most part doomed to failure since all the requirements for success were missing. "I have watched Dr. Gall spread out the brain like a handkerchief," explained Müller, "but I have learned nothing about mental illness," and Cox reasoned that the findings of anatomists might give rise to the notion that the brain had little to do with the mind. There is a prophetic ring to the words of Jacobi (1834), who rejected the help of Reil's "psychologists": "It would have been more practical to seek instead a competent anatomist or an expert chemist, for the director of such a large institution will scarcely find time to perform necessary anatomical explorations and chemical analyses; on the other hand, there is nothing to hamper someone else from carrying out these tasks under his direction and at his bidding." Many decades were to pass before his wish was fulfilled. Finally, Blumröder deserves credit for suggesting that the microscope and chemical analysis could be used to great advantage in pathological anatomy.

Revealed by post-mortem examinations were deviations in the skull bones and meninges, vascular diseases, different degrees of cerebral plethora, changes in the weight, size and density of the brain, dilation of brain cavities, brain damage, mollification, pus, tumors, inflammations. Particular attention was paid to calcaceous deposits around the pineal gland, formations of bubbles in the vascular plexuses in brain cavities, variations in color, softening or hardening of brain tissue. Physical changes—bleeding, palor, putrefaction—were doubtlessly often associated with manifestations of particular diseases. Chiarugi noted that he had found that blood vessels in the brains of deranged, delirious, and babbling lunatics were often filled with air. Vering added that brain cavities were sometimes empty, sometimes filled with humors.

It is obvious that under these circumstances any attempt to understand insanity on the basis of post-mortem examinations was certain to entail disappointment. Knight, who thought that he had generally found in mental patients "an appreciable enlargement of the blood vessels and an inordinate diffusion of blood," nevertheless explained that in dissecting the body of a mental patient he had never observed a change that he had not often observed in dissecting the body of a sane patient. Esquirol and Jacobi were of the same opinion. Neumann also remarked that it was often impossible during an autopsy to detect any trace of an unhealthy change in the brain. Against this, a post-mortem examination might reveal that the brain of an individual who had appeared while alive to be perfectly sane was actually sickly or had been almost totally destroyed or even injured by a foreign body long before death occurred. Zeller stated as late as 1848: "If we ask ourselves whether observations and research in the field of pathological anatomy have actually contributed significantly to our understanding of mental disease (as many people claim they have), the answer is no." It is to such study, however, that we owe one of the great discoveries in our field—the definition of progressive paralysis by Bayle and Calmeil in 1820. Their studies show that researchers were groping in the dark, however, when they tried to relate symptoms to deposits of "brain dust" around the pineal gland or to fine vascular networks near the protruding surfaces of the brain ("chords") to which Bergmann attributed great importance. It was also hoped that new light would be shed on the nature of insanity by changes in the viscera, especially the intestine and other organs in the abdominal region, as well as by the condition of separate organs in comparison with each other.

Progress was first made possible by microscopic examination of healthy and diseased brains. Earlier Chiarugi after reporting that often even the most careful examination failed to reveal any appreciable change in the brain of a lunatic, had surmised that "a modification, though imperceptible, might still be present and capable in spite of its insignificance of interfering with psychic processes." Even in Gudden's time, however, little importance was attached to the search for modifications in brain tissue among the mentally ill. The decisive step was the development of the technique of preparing stained slides for microscopic examination. This technique, largely the contribution of Nissl and Weigert, enabled researchers to examine in detail the different types of tissue in the brain and to study minute modifications. It also opened up new and unanticipated fields of research by making it possible to identify and separate diverse effects produced by disease. Through their untiring, methodical efforts originators of the technique (Nissl and Alzheimer) and their countless students finally provided a basis for a medical explanation of the morbific processes that culminate in insanity. We have firm ground under our feet in only a few tiny areas and cannot be certain that our present resources will enable us to solve all the problems that confront us, but we have joined forces with those working in other fields of medicine and our concerted efforts will doubtlessly meet with success. Research with animals has been most fruitful since here many diseases can be studied under simplified conditions and their progress charted. The same processes could be studied in human beings only during certain phases and under complicated conditions.

We hope through research to achieve an understanding of what goes on in the cortex during the course of different disorders, to identify the conditions that produced them, and to separate them from each other. But all this would still not complete our task. Even more important in the study of psychic disorders produced by a disease is the extent and nature of the affected area of the brain. We can be certain that the inordinately complicated structure of the brain is closely related to its function of continuously combining countless images that differ in form, quality and arrangement with an infinite number of particular performances. Our last objective, still far beyond our reach, is to acquaint ourselves with the number, type and significance of the separate parts that function jointly in the unified system of the brain and to be able whenever a disorder occurs to infer the seat and extent of the morbific changes that have caused it.

Progress in this direction was not easy. Not surprisingly, at first researchers were guided by completely arbitrary assumptions. Neumann reported that Schellhammer wrongly identified intelligence with gray matter and both judgment and perception with the largest areas of the hemispheres. Willis placed the power of imagination in the corpus callosum cerebri, the emotions in the two frontal regions, the instincts in the pineal gland. Laneisi placed the faculty of judgment in the pineal gland. Glaser thought that memory had its seat in the cerebellum. "We can easily see," added Neumann, "that there was no basis for any of these suppositions." Haindorf surmised that the spinal column was the seat of "brute complacency," that the cerebrum was the seat of the psyche, and that the cerebellum was the "organ of concentration and feeling" since it had the most complicated and complete organization, the most distinct articulation, a round and therefore near-perfect shape and no out-going nerves, making it a self-contained entity.

Schröder van der Kolk identified the occipital and parietal regions as the seat of emotions, the frontal region as that of the intellect. Blumröder explained that the cerebellum was the "individual brain" (in contrast to the "divine brain" or cerebrum), "the active, sanguinary, Ahriman brain" (a blind impulse in contrast to judicious reflection, the hallmark of the cerebrum). Guislain attempted to relate the emotions to the parietal and the temporal region. Bergmann made all sorts of arbitrary associations between particular psychic activities and his "chord" system.

The study of the skull which Gall and Spurzheim initiated had resulted at the beginning of the eighteenth century in the delineation of a number of regions on the surface of the brain, each of them supposed to be the seat of a particular faculty. The method introduced by Gall consisted in correlating prominent regions of the brains of animals with outstanding psychic traits and in examining the skulls of men with exceptional abilities, talents or deficiencies and correlating bumps and depressions found at various points with one of those characteristics. The objections that would inevitably be raised against such a method are apparent. In the first place, the surface of the skull does not accurately indicate the structure of the brain; moreover, the convolutions of the brain have nothing to do with the protrusion of the hemispheres. Even more important, the positing of a correlation between the shape of the brain and mental traits was completely arbitrary and unscientific, and the arbitrarily selected mental faculties were so complex that they could not be localized in a circumscribed region of the brain.

Later researchers therefore considered Gall's assertion false. Indeed, for a while even the concept of a correlation of certain activities with specific parts of the brain was rejected. Research with animals led Flourens to conclude that damage to the brain resulted in general, not specific impairment of mental activities. His conclusion was suddenly invalidated when Fritsch and Hitzig (1870) succeeded in eliciting convulsive movements in separate muscles through electrical stimulation of specific points on the surface of the brain. There are arguments both for and against linking cerebral activities closely to circumscribed areas of the brain. Although every complicated process necessarily presupposes the concerted action of many different organs, evidence now favors the affirmative side. The most telling arguments are the fact that in human beings the destruction of the third left frontal convolution (Broca's area) entails aphasia, Wernicke's brilliant discovery that the seat of the linguistic faculty is in the upper left temporal convolution, and corroborating Munk's research with animals, proof that in man, too, sight is directly linked to specific areas of the occipital cortex. Thus the cerebral cortex was eventually partitioned into separate regions, each supposedly responsible for certain activities. Flechsing later was able on the basis of phylogeny to delineate a number of cortical regions which he classed as sensory or associative centers.

All these attempts to discover the seat of specific mental

Manfred Sakel

activities were hampered by neglect of the structure of the cortex. Meynert had already described not only its successive layers but also certain differences between layers in separate regions. If we assume that deviations in their structure are matched by certain mental deviations, it follows that the cortex could have no such unity as that suggested by cartographic classifications; we have to reckon separate regions that not only lie in spatial juxtaposition but also overlap and interpenetrate. This viewpoint is strongly supported by the investigations of Voigt and Brodmann, who in the Neurobiological Institute first studied differences between the successive strata of the cortex. They showed that the organ of our mental life consists of a great number of stratified structures which vary in size and make-up; they also showed that in animals the same structures exhibit significant phylogenetic differences with respect to both their extension and their relation to each other. It is apparently in these structures that we must seek the forces responsible for the simple mental deviations that jointly mediate every conscious act. So far, however, we have been able to identify only a few of these structures with specific activities.

The etiology of insanity profited but little from the progress of science, mainly because no serious attempt was made to relate a particular type of insanity to a specific cause. This was due in part to the absence of any clear-cut definition of the different types; classification was generally accomplished on the basis of symptoms alone, not the underlying processes responsible for the disease. Thus even in the systems of men like Meynert and Wernicke etiological considerations were brushed aside. Of course wherever there was a causal relation between an injury and the occurence of insanity, its type was identified with its cause. Causal influences are often complex and their role hard to assess. We are nevertheless able in many instances to infer the cause of a disease from its symptoms.

The greatest step toward understanding the etiology of mental disease was the discovery that paresis resulted from syphilis. Individual researchers first suspected the syphilitic origin of the fatal disease, and their hypothesis was gradually strengthened by later findings. The Wassermann reaction in the blood serum and spinal fluid, together with the discovery of morbific agents in the brain, today offer convincing proof. Still to be answered, however, is the question of the exact nature of causal relations, for other syphilitic diseases of the brain differ radically from paresis.

Recent research in syphilis, especially the priceless discovery of the Wassermann reaction, have cast light on the importance of the dreadful affliction to psychiatry. We can expect this light to illuminate still other spheres of our science. As a rule we gradually come to understand something about unfamiliar diseases by working with a number of patients and can then explain many cases that we have previously misunderstood; in the same way patient, methodical research in the field of feeblemindedness, whether congenital or acquired early in life, should complement what is now known about the influence of syphilis. The same probably applies to many congenital defects, especially degenerative diseases. Bringing these conditions to light is important since their revelation also enhances our ability to combat them.

A second important etiological discovery was recently made. Though less spectacular than the first, its long-term possibilities hold even greater promise. It involves the influence of the thyroid gland on mental and physical health, first explained mainly through the efforts of Kocher. Abnormal secretion or the absence of secretion can produce serious, even fatal disorders that follow a characteristic course: hyperactivity of the thyroid gland causes exophthalmic goiter (Basedow's disease); inactivity causes myxedema in adults and cretinism in children. Remarkable results in the treatment of cretinism have already been made possible by our knowledge, and these results give rise to the hope that this and other medical advances will gradually eliminate the scourge of the Alps. Even more important, the example of the thyroid gland drew the attention of researchers to a long list of other glands and their activities. It can even be said that our whole conception of the mechanism of the body has been influenced by their findings. Although the role of each of these glands is more complex than that of the thyroid, researchers have already completed numerous experiments which have added to our knowledge of developmental disorders.

Closely resembling glandular disorders are those relating to metabolism. In many types of insanity, especially those characterized by marked changes in weight, we can be certain that they are of capital importance. Urinalysis, long the mainstay of reserarchers, proved wholly inadequate to the task of illuminating the many constitutional deviations which they presumed to examine. Recently perfected metabolism tests, on the other hand, seem to hold great promise in the case of epilepsy, paralysis, manic-depressive psychosis, and dementia praecox. Piecemeal results reported to date suggest that valuable information will be gleaned from the study of every aspect of metabolism. Even more valuable information may one day be supplied by incisive reasearch in serology. The dialytic process raised high hopes in the field of psychiatry, but they are still unrealized. It seems nevertheless that the key to understanding many vital processes, both normal and abnormal, is to be sought in the make-up of the blood and the cells, and that it will also be possible for our science to advance persistently and methodically along the avenues now being opened.

Profound changes have marked the development of our theory of the physical causes and bases of insanity. Though our attitude toward the influence of psychic forces on the development of mental disorders has changed but slightly, our assessment of their importance has fluctuated. While the old psychic school assigned them a dominant role, the somatic school tended to consider them unimportant. Popular opinion steadfastly championed the importance of psychic influences in the etiology of insanity, and even Griesinger held that they were generally more decisive than physical injuries. Today we have apparently arrived at a clear-cut definition. We know that frequently so-called psychic causes—unhappy love, failure in business, overwork— are the product rather than the cause of the disease, that they are but the outward manifestation of a pre-existing condition, and finally, that their effects depend for the most part on the subject's anlage. Doubtlessly, however, mental disorders that make up one clearly defined group do have a psychic origin. The most important of these, generally brought to light by strong emotions, are the hysterical disorders known to us since Charcot and Mobius, accident neuroses (following the enactment of compensation laws) and, closely related to the latter, combat neuroses.

Often decisive in the etiology of insanity is the role of the individual's native endowment, especially as it is determined by heredity. Hereditary defects were noted by the first alienists; also noted was the fact that not only severe mental disorders but also various types of related defects or pernicious conditions can be transmitted from parent to offspring. It was soon obvious that hereditary factors were transmitted to successive generations and that they could be expressed in collateral lines. Researchers naturally made many attempts to estimate the incidence of hereditary mental disorders, and in each instance any defective condition that could be discovered figured indiscriminately in their calculations. As we might expect, the numerical values that they established varied with the quality of their research and the weight assigned to particular assertions, with the result that estimates differed enormously and produced a beclouded picture of the role of hereditary factors in different types of insanity. Not until recently was any attempt made to compare insane individuals and sane individuals with hereditary defects. As the investigations of Diem have shown, many hereditary defects are transmitted but not to all offspring. Strong compensatory forces must be at work in the hereditary process, for in the absence of reinforcement from some other source successive blood mixtures tend to dilute a defective anlage. This observation discredited the theory of Morel, who had described the transmission of degenerative disorders to increasing numbers of individuals through successive generations and exerted a profound influence on psychiatry in France, and encouraged Magnan and others to compare the mental disorders of degenerates with those of normally endowed individuals. Though their efforts have illuminated the close ties between certain types of insanity and hereditary anlage, no one has succeeded in separating hereditary and nonhereditary types.

One important issue that could not be resolved until

more had been learned about the basic pattern of each of a number of disorders was the influence of hereditary on a particular type of mental disease. Earlier it was assumed that when transmitted through heredity a generally defective anlage could result in the appearance of particular defects. Recent investigations, among which those of Pilcz are the most exhaustive, have shown that specific diseases are hereditary even though diverse influences often veil the close link between the condition of the parent and that of the offspring. To be considered here as in all studies of inheritance is the difference, emphasized for the first time only recently, between hereditary defects in the strict sense and contamination. The first applies to the transmission of inherited parental defects, the second to the transmission of a pernicious condition acquired in some way by one parent.

The pioneering investigations of Mendel have raised wholly new issues in the science of heredity. Psychiatry is also compelled by the discovery of the laws of inheritance to research these issues from new and better vantage points. It is our task, following the example set by Rudin, to identify the specific laws that govern the transmission of diverse traits associated with insanity and wherever possible to illuminate the conditions under which there first appears the germ of a disease that can be transmitted from parent to offspring. We can be sure that the answer to our questions will be revealed through patient, methodical study of long lines of descent and that brilliant minds will one day harvest the fruits of research initiated now. There would be nothing to harvest, however, if no one saw fit to sow.

We have come to the edge of new fields of research. Only the distant future will reveal the process through which external circumstances and innate traits interact to produce a diversity of symptoms. Piecemeal investigations have already indicated that the symptomology of a disease varies with the individual's age, sex, race and hereditary anlage. Comparative psychiatrists would provide new insight into the nature and etiology of insanity by adding to our knowledge of relevant factors and by identifying influences formerly considered indiscriminately. Our science will also profit from demographic studies. Carefully planned censuses will enable us to study processes and changes among the population. They will provide us with information concerning the incidence of mild and severe mental disorders and, more important still, concerning the still unanswered and fateful question of whether they are constantly increasing.

A most decisive influence on the history of psychiatry was the competency of alienists and the evolution of an independent discipline relating to the treatment of the mentally ill. It was reported that on May 24, 1789 Pinel with the permission of the national assembly removed the chains from 49 lunatics; the scene was recently depicted in a painting by the artist Robert-Fleury. Though Lahr inferred that the account was pure invention, the fact remains that mental patients were freed from their chains by doctors. Several decades passed, however, before this advance resulted in truly humane treatment of lunatics. Esquirol reported that occasionally restraining jackets which he had introduced to replace chains were rejected by institutions because chains were cheaper. Corporal punishment gradually disappeared along with chains but was long considered indispensable as a training device and as an instrument for combating the evil tendencies of patients.

Chains were gradually replaced by other, less brutal restraining devices and by instruments of torture designed to revive and redirect ravaged minds. Several decades were to pass, however, before the conviction that chains were useless and cruel permanently banished this spectre from most institutions. As late as 1834 Leuret recommended that cold douches be used to "intimidate" patients, to combat their disagreeable practices, and to rid them of their delusions. Mainly, however, physical restraint was used to protect others from dangerous patients.

Credit for having cleared the way for the elimination of this practice in institutions for the insane goes to English alienists—Gardiner Hill, Charlesworth, and especially Conolly. On September 21, 1839 Conolly, encouraged by the experience of the other two doctors, dared to remove all restraining instruments from Hanwell. The experiment was remarkably successful in that great institution for the insane, but only because, as Conolly never tired of repeating, a complete revolution in the handling and care of patients was simultaneously executed. Instead of using physical restraint to repress external manifestations of disorders, he had to find some means of exerting a favorable influence on the mental life of patients, preventing accidents, and eliminating evil tendencies or diverting them into harmless channels. Conolly achieved all this by giving patients comfortable accommodations, conscientiously caring for their needs, treating them sympathetically, consoling them, familiarizing himself with their individual problems, and providing them with appropriate activities and diversions. He observed that patients were far less dangerous than they had earlier appeared; indeed, that many unpleasant, obstructive, and dangerous traits had actually been the product of the

Julius Wagner-Jauregg

treatment intended forcibly to suppress the symptoms of their disease. As in the fable of the contest between the sun and the wind for the traveler's coat, the warm sun of human love quickly achieved what was beyond the reach of brutal force.

It is clear that this innovation could not have been accomplished without the active, dedicated and understanding co-operation of the hospital staff. Heinroth had already noted that service personnel in institutions for the insane should be "strong, healthy, fearless, skilled men who are sympathetic, zealous, and open-minded enough first to assimilate and put to use all sorts of skills and concepts associated with the treatment of mental disorders, and second to adapt themselves to the peculiarities of the patients. They ought to be neither irritable and emotional nor phlegmatic and lazy; neither drowsy nor drunk. They must have a good, clean appearance. Since patients are, as it were, placed in their trust, attendants must try to win their trust and respect through friendliness, thoughtfulness and firmness."

Some means had to be found for improving the competency of attendants in the performance of their difficult tasks. Alienists are still searching, with varying success, for the right approach. It was necessary first of all to offer salaries that would attract capable workers, then to prepare them for their work by giving them adequate training and to provide them with insurance, a retirement program, recreational facilities, and the opportunity to enjoy a normal family life. Efforts to improve conditions were facilitated by the gradual disappearance of abuses and dangers that had previously made the attendant's task unbearable. Regular classes and practical examinations helped to some extent to prepare workers efficiently to discharge their duties. Nursing is now held in such high repute that almost every institution for the insane male patients can be attended by nurses; a century ago it was held that male attendants were required even in the case of female patients.

The change brought about by the gradual disappearance of restraining devices is almost inconceivable. Their disappearance eventually entailed that of the deep-rooted tendency to punish patients in some way for their misconduct. New regulations were intended not to draw attention to the impropriety of their conduct but to eliminate dangers and unwholesome conditions. Institutions became homes in which patients enjoyed maximum freedom: restrictions were only for the protection of the individual and his fellow sufferers. This change of viewpoint had a profound effect on the conduct of inmates and on the institution as a whole. Patients became calmer and were more tractable, felt secure in their surroundings and submitted willingly to the measures used to alleviate their suffering. They were also more responsive to the doctor's instructions. The persistent battle waged by many mental patients against their loss of freedom and against their presumed oppressors now lost much of its bitterness after physical force and punitive measures were abandoned.

In spite of these obvious advantages, the movement initiated by Conolly made slow progress, mainly because it was first necessary to devise new measures to replace the use of force. In Germany Ludwig Meyer was the first (1862) to take the decisive step of rejecting the use of restraining devices. But the battle over this innovation endured for decades until finally people became convinced that coercive measures, with few exceptions, were unnecessary and therefore objectionable. During the last thirty years I have examined thousands of patients; only one of them, a confused, highly excitable epileptic, had to be tied to his bed with towels for a few days to prevent fatal bleeding.

To take the place of restraining devices Conolly recommended putting severely disturbed patients in a padded cell for a short time. The "isolation" or brief confinement of patients in blockhouses, cells, and other such places is still considered indispensable by many alienists and in all probably represent a major failure in our attempt to devise a better system. In Germany the first improvement over the dungeon was the stockade devised by Autenrieth. Stoves and windows were protected against their attacks by thick boards, with the results that patients could be allowed freedom of movement. Heinroth criticized this very feature, saying that the will had to be restrained since it contained the very essence of the patient's disease. Subsequently padded cells were often introduced only to be abandoned when filth made them unbearable. Every institution therefore was equipped with a number of isolation rooms distinguished by their carefully secured windows and doors, by floors, walls and ceilings that could be washed easily, and by the absence of anything that might enable the patient to hurt himself. The accommodations were of course uncomfortable; with the possible exception of an immovable table, all furnishings were excluded. Straw brought in for the occasion and covered with strong sailcloth often served as a bed; it was frequently necessary, however, to strip dangerous patients and give them nothing except some straw or seaweed.

Isolation led to a long, hard struggle between the ingenuity of doctors and technicians and the destructive inclination of patients. The latter were the ultimate victors. There was no effective way to combat the destructive, suicidal and obscene tendencies of patients placed in isolation. Furthermore, apart from all the other difficulties that it raised, isolation was apparently responsible for the dangerous tendencies that gave rise to the degenerate, bestial "institutional artifacts" which were the bane of every alienist. Such shameful conditions usually developed only after long confinement, but the practice, once it had been initiated, was always easy to extend and hard to retrench. It would be a mistake to assume that isolation normally eliminates unhealthy symptoms; it merely conceals them and rules out careful supervision and treatment. Moreover, in many instances the patient can be placed in isolation only after he has been forcibly subdued.

Under such conditions alienists could not fail to try to restrict insofar as possible the evil of isolation. Attempts to eliminate it altogether gradually made headway. Wattenberg, Heilbronner and Hoppe energetically set about the task of perfecting a "cell-less" system of treatment. Today we can be sure that the renunciation of confinement is possible and that it is a significant step toward changing lunatic asylums into convalescent homes. I have been able to desipense with isolation for the last fifteen years and believe that it could be eliminated in large institutions if all patients were henceforth treated differently. Proper treatment is costly, however, and can not be provided in all institutions; prime requirements are competent medical care, a large staff of well-trained attendants, and spacious wards.

An important step toward proper treatment was the practice of keeping patients under constant surveillance (first advocated by Parchappe) and confining newly admitted patients to their beds (first used systematically by Guislain in treating melancholia). At first only those with physical injuries, invalids, and cripples seemed to require such confinement. Gradually the situation changed and more and more new patients were placed in special wards and confined, exclusively or part of the time, to their beds. The result was that the most offensive symptoms vanished almost altogether. Ill-humored patients were less resentful; excitable patients became calm; stubborn patients became more tractable; they gained weight. These experiences clearly proved to the doctor that the sick brain, like every other unhealthy organ, needs rest agove all else. Patients became calmer and less obstructive; the atmosphere of the insane asylum became more like that of a regular hospital.

Providing patients with beds in wards enabled them to receive incomparably better supervision and care. A relatively small number of attendants could watch over a great number of patients day and night. Timely intervention prevented countless offenses, disorders and dangers; self-inflicted injuries and accidents decreased; it was much easier to care for uncleanly, sickly and undernourished patients. Because of its great advantages bed treatment, instituted and energetically advocated by Neisser, soon was widely adopted in Germany. In other countries, however, progress was slow. Today every good institution in Germany has spacious wards in which not only new patients but also veteran inmates whose symptoms flare up anew can find rest and specialized care. In municipal asylums for new patients, bed treatment is a rule, and the rule is relaxed only for convalescents and for chronic patients.

Once bed treatment had significantly restricted seclusion of patients, a further step forward could be accomplished. This was the increased use of warm baths and especially of protracted baths. The older doctors had often praised the soothing effect of warm baths; in the 1840s Brierre de Boismont had kept patients in baths equipped with sprays from 6 to 14 hours. In recent times Scholz, especially, has often placed patients for long periods in canvas-covered bathtubs. This practice was restricted not only by its cost but also by the fear of its debilitating effects and sudden heart failure. After experience during the last decade had shown that protracted baths, even if continued for several days or weeks, had few adverse effects on patients, they became indispensable therapeutic adjuvants in Germany. Their greatest advantage is that in the average institution they render isolation unnecessary and therefore facilitate the constant supervision of all patients. They effectively control stormy outbursts and greatly reduce the evil of uncleanliness and the urge to destroy. Finally, they minimize the danger of bedsores among invalids and cripples, always difficult to prevent if bed patients are unclean.

We should not fail to note that the solution of many difficulties faced by the older doctors is the contribution of the chemical industry which in the last decade has created an imposing list of new soporifics and sedatives. The first sedative was chloral hydrate, recommended by Liebreich. Almost every other drug with similar effects was first manufactured and administered in Germany. Such agents are rightly considered expedients, however, and their use opens the door to many dangers. Still, for countless patients they are an immeasurable blessing, and they are mainly responsible for bringing the quiet atmosphere of the hospital into wards for the insane and removing much of the horror that still feeds the imagination of the lay public.

Finally we should note that the overall progress scored by medical science has contributed in many different ways to the improvement of medical practice in institutions for the insane. Apart from preventive measures with respect to widespread contagious diseases and efficacious treatment of all types of physical ailments, particularly with the help of new advances in surgery, two contributions stand out: Pravaz's syringe and Gummi's stomach-probe. Both instruments have become very important in the treatment of mental patients. They have enabled us for the first time to circumvent the patient's resistance to the intake of medicine and food. With them we are able in many instances quickly and effectively to promote relaxation and to restore physical strength; formerly nothing seemed to be of any help.

All these revolutionary changes within institutions for the insane entailed profound changes in their external appearance and even in their structure. At the beginning of the nineteenth century an attempt had been made to separate custodial mental hospitals and active treatment centers. Damerow urged that the two be partially merged by the spatial grafting of the second to the first. It was soon learned that an immediate decision on the prognosis of a patient was often impossible, that the number of incurable patients in hospitals quickly soared, and that occasionally unexpected cures were effected in custodial institutions. The result was that many incurable patients became valuable, even indispensable components in the life of the hospital and that the transfer of a patient from one center to the other was a cruel experience for him and his family. All these considerations eventually led to the adoption of our present viewpoint: patients should be grouped according to their condition and their needs rather than according to the nature of their disease and the prospect of their recovering.

Since curable patients are normally released sooner or later, incurable patients necessarily predominate in institutions for the insane. A new viewpoint therefore emerges: in caring for patients emphasis should be placed on preserving and putting to the best possible use their damaged mental faculties. This goal can best be reached by keeping patients occupied, as the old alienists had emphatically recommended. It was realized in Reil's program in which the insane asylum was modeled on a farm; it was also advocated in France, especially by Ferrus. Thus it was that institutions frequently included shops and gardens, and even more often fields and stables. In many places there were small colonies in which quiet, capable patients could enjoy considerable freedom and independence while pursuing worthy occupations.

The favorable influence of such institutions on patients was obvious. All such undertakings required careful planning. Outstanding was Koppe's success in making the Alterscherbitz manor a vital part of a large institution for the insane. From 1876 on, the operation of the estate took first place in the life of the institution; every attempt was made to provide patients with the maximum degree of freedom consonant with their circumstances. This first large-scale experiment, which was remarkably successful, was the prototype of a vast number of similar "colonial" institutions, especially in Germany. Though such institutions necessarily varied in detail according to the character of the population, there can be no doubt that healthful

Josef Breuer

Sigmund Freud

occupations benefit most able-bodied patients more than anything else.

The attempt to provide patients with a maximum of freedom of movement and with the opportunity to engage in worthwhile pursuits naturally entailed the elimination of those features that gave asylums the appearance of prisons or barracks. Monstrous buildings were replaced by numbers of smaller units; the design of these buildings, much like farmhouses, was determined by the needs of different types of patients. Thus the asylum with its varied buildings scattered irregularly in gardens and pleasure-grounds took on the appearance of a small estate or village, especially since a few old farm buildings were used to house individual patients. An effort was made insofar as possible to eliminate anything that might serve as a reminder of the special function of the institution. The walls that surrounded the old asylum gave way to simple fences or hedges and lattices were removed from windows except where their retention was absolutely necessary. Massive doors also disappeared wherever it was possible to allow patients the freedom of the institutional grounds. We scarcely need mention that inside the different houses, stress was placed on comfort, homeliness and good taste.

A great number of technical advances also played a part in making modern institutions wholly unlike the old. We can hardly imagine the conditions that existed in the old institutions in the absence of plumbing and sewage pipes; there was no hot water in the kitchen, none for washing; oil lamps and tallow candles were the only sources of light; heat was supplied by inefficient hot-air pipes or by a grilled stove; windows were protected from the attacks of enraged patients by thick gratings; there were no telephones to provide prompt communication at all times between different areas.

The revolution that occurred during the course of a century shows up clearly in the development of psychiatric methods in Munich. The old "lunatic cells" with their rings and chains in the first hospital were replaced in 1801 by 25 rooms in the asylum built by Griesinger. The asylum was soon notorious and so over-crowded that patients could not even be segregated according to sex. These conditions led in 1859 to the erection of a district asylum, later enlarged several times, which on April 1, 1860 accommodated 166 patients. The asylum was first directed by Solbrig, then by Gudden. Each of the four sections of the barracks-type structure was enclosed by a square garden. By 1877, the number of usable rooms had surpassed 500. When it too became overcrowded, the construction of the colonial-type Gabersee institution was undertaken. The old institution was finally abandoned altogether. It was replaced in 1905 by Eglfing's large rural asylum, to which the Haar institution was annexed in 1912. On January 1, 1917 the three institutions in Upper Bavaria and the psychiatric clinic erected in 1904 accommodated a grand total of 2,751 patients. This represents an increase of 1,657 per cent over a period of 57 years.

The final topic in our survey of the evolution of psychiatry is family nursing, or the accommodation of selected patients in their own homes or in the homes of strangers under professional supervision. The pattern for family nursing was set by the Belgian village of Gheel. For centuries Gheel had been the mecca of mental patients in search of a cure. That is how a number of patients came to find lodging in private homes. In spite of many drawbacks, this type of treatment had so many good features that it was later imitated elsewhere. In Germany it was first adopted, more than a century ago, in Rockwinckel. It was not widely adopted in Germany, however, until the last few decades. Nowadays it is practiced with varying degrees of success in many different localities. Wherever the local population is suited to the practice, it is doubtlessly much better to entrust the care of the patient to a family rather than to place him in an institution. With the family he can enjoy full freedom of movement, worthy employment and familiar surroundings. Patients must be carefully selected, however, and placed under the constant supervision of a physician.

But today concern for the welfare of our patients does not end when they are discharged by the physician. The last several decades have witnessed the formation of benevolent associations in many places to help discharged patients. Most of them have been patterned after the one founded in Heppenheim by Ludwig. Their task is to facilitate the return of patients who have recovered or improved to a normal pattern of living, to help them with their problems, and by so doing, to preserve and fortify the good results achieved through institutional treatment. Equally important is the fact that these benevolent associations through their activities have narrowed the gap between institutional doctors and laymen, gradually weakened deep-rooted prejudices against asylums, and brought to the attention of a wider audience our obligations to our fellow men who suffer from mental disease. The same effects have resulted from greater accessibility to institutions for the insane on the part of the outside world; contributory factors have been the disappearance of surrounding walls, the performance of ordinary farm tasks by patients, provisions for greater freedom of movement, and cordiality toward visitors.

If we compare the situation of mental patients today with the circumstances that prevailed a century ago, the revolution that has been accomplished comes into clear focus. The words penned by Nostiz in 1829 ring true: "If we weigh objectively the accomplishments of the last half century and try to determine how far we are in theory, word and deed from our goal, then we may reasonably conclude that the progress now being made in psychiatry and the uses to which it is now being put in our institutions will result in its complete transformation before the end of the present century." One by one prejudices have been overcome, abuses and cruel practices eliminated, new means found to alleviate mental diseases. Spearheading this advance was the growing body of scientific knowledge relating to the nature and etiology of insanity and deriving from study of data in different fields of investigation and from the overall progress of the science of medicine. Unrelenting effort on the part of a large number of alienists gradually transformed the sad lot of the mentally ill, with the result that today we are actually nearing the end of our struggle. To be sure there are still many defects to be remedied and improvements to be made, but we are not being presumptuous in stating that we have discovered the approach to be followed henceforth in psychiatry.

Our satisfaction over the progress already made is tinged with regret. When we consider the extraordinary sacrifices made by those responsible for the evolution of psychiatry, we are constrained to lament the fact that all the hopes tied to it can never be fulfilled. We must openly admit that the vast majority of the patients placed in our institutions are according to what we know forever lost, that even the best of care can never restore them to perfect health. Our treatment probably makes life endurable for a vast number of mental cripples whose plight would otherwise be intolerable, but only rarely does it effect a cure. A study made at the request of Vocke showed that out of 1,183 patients in Eglfing on January 1, 1917, no less than 826, or 70%, were considered incurable. This should come as no surprise to anyone with psychiatric experience. Also to be considered is the fact that patients who recovered were always discharged while incurable patients accumulated; thus it is obvious that by itself even the best psychiatric therapy can not eradicate the scourge of mental disease.

We must therefore ask if there are other, more promising, approaches. The answer is a resounding yes. Most promising is the prevention of insanity, though this is possible today only to the extent that we are acquainted with the causes of the affliction and are capable of combating it. We know the basic causes of three major diseases: hereditary defects, alcoholism, and syphilis. They constitute, according to the most conservative estimates, at least one third of all mental disorders treated in our clinic. Then comes addiction to morphine and cocaine. Traumatic neuroses can also be prevented. An autocrat in possession of our present knowledge would be able, if he showed no consideration for the lifelong habits of men, to effect a significant reduction in the incidence of insanity within a few decades. We can entertain even higher hopes. The nature of most mental disorders is now obscured. But no one will deny that further research will uncover new facts in so young a science as ours; in this respect the diseases produced by syphilis are an object lesson. It is logical to assume that we shall succeed in uncovering the causes of many other types of insanity that can be prevented—perhaps even cured—though at present we have not the slightest clue; a case in point was cretinism before the discovery of the thyroid treatment.

Only scientific research can bring about the realization of such advances. In the past it has spearheaded medical advances, and on it will depend our success in the future. It is not, as might be assumed, the favorite pastime of a few enlightened minds but the basis for all further progress. The great war in which we are now engaged has compelled us to recognize the fact that science could forge for us a host of effective weapons for use against a hostile world. Should it be otherwise if we are fighting an internal enemy seeking to destroy the very fabric of our existence? Hardenberg said in his decree of February 16, 1805: "The state must concern itself with all institutions for those with damaged minds, both for the betterment of the unfortunates and for the advancement of science. In this important and difficult field of medicine only unrelenting efforts will enable us to carve out advances for the good of suffering mankind. Perfection can be achieved only in such institutions; here are found all the conditions necessary for conducting experiments to test basic theories and for using the results of such experimentation for the advancement of science."

Anyone familiar with the present state of our science will see that further advancement will require measures not now in use. The nature of psychiatry is such that questions which are constantly being formulated can be answered only on the basis of evidence supplied by a number of auxiliary disciplines; clinical observation must be supplemented by thorough examination of healthy and diseased brains, neurology, the study of heredity and

Alfred Adler

degenerative diseases, the chemistry of metabolism, and serology. Only exceptionally well-trained specialists possess competency in each particular field; their ranks are thin and, because of unfavorable external conditions, they now have only a limited opportunity to exercise their skills. These observations clearly show that only a well-planned and comprehensive program of research can bring us closer to the goal which we are striving to attain. We ought therefore to note with pride and satisfaction that it was possible for us in Germany in the middle of a raging war to take the first step toward establishing a research institute for the purpose of determining the nature of mental diseases and of discovering techniques for effecting their prevention, alleviation and cure. All those who have contributed to the success of this great undertaking, especially His Majesty our King and the worthy authors of the program, merit our most cordial thanks. A far greater recompense than anything which we might be able to say today, however, is the hope that ground has already been broken for new approaches that will enable us to win a victory over the direst afflictions that can beset man.

But we have taken only the first step toward our goal. Even under the most favorable conditions, the fruits of scientific labor generally ripen very slowly, and in our field quick, dazzling results are unthinkable; quite apart from these considerations, providing funds for the elaboration of a unified program of research poses a challenge still to be faced. We believe that we can face it with confidence. The cost of providing psychiatric care is staggering; efforts to lower costs, if promising, should receive unqualified support. According to figures supplied by Vocke, a large research institute could be operated on an annual budget of 200,000 marks, or one-tenth of one per cent of the total funds now required for the operation of our institutions. If each year the research institute succeeded only in preventing mental disease in one out of 1,000 cases or in helping one out of 1,000 inmates to regain his freedom, it follows that the expense of the institute would soon be recovered. Can we ignore such important considerations? It seems to me that we should recall here the words used by Müller in 1824 to reject the notion that attempts to better the situation of the insane might be impeded by the impossibility of raising the necessary funds. "In this wide world," he said, "there are still many unmarried and childless men whose coffers have been richly blessed and whose sense of charity, which is not dead but merely dormant, needs to be awakened and guided toward this beautiful, sacred goal. And what goal could be more sacred than that of caring for a brother in distress, especially when the affliction is distinctly human and therefore more obvious than others, and when it respects neither reason nor rank nor riches?"

EPILOGUE

In this essay on the early history of psychiatry, Professor Emil Kraepelin, "the father of psychiatry," brilliantly summarizes the progress made in our field following rejection of the notion that mental illness was linked to the consequences of sin.

The move from humid dungeons where troublesome psychotics were chained to the walls into modern hospitals has revolutionized psychiatry. Euphemistic terms were used to conceal the nature and purposes of many of the older items. Thus the strait-jacket was called a camisole, the seclusion room an isolation area; the rough canvas stretched over a steel frame to immobilize hyperactive and assaultive patients from head to foot was termed a restraining sheet. Brutal guards were not allowed to use these devices indiscriminately and threateningly; they were used only under the supervision of the physician.

By 1917, however, when Kraepelin wrote his essay, most hospital care for the sufferer from psychosis and disabling psychoneurosis was strictly custodial. Shelter, food, clothing and moderately kind supervision contributed the major part of the treatment; barbiturates, chloral hydrate, hyoscine and hydrotherapy were used as adjuvants in cases of dangerous excited states.

Since 1917 an encouraging change has been taking place in the care of the mentally ill. The main reasons for this change are the following:

1) Impressive advances have been made in the *somatic treatment of psychiatric illness*.
    a) Wagner-Jauregg's malarial treatment for general paresis (1917)
    b) Manfred Sakel's insulin treatment for schizophrenia (1927)
    c) Meduna's metrazol shock treatment (1928) and Cerletti and Bini's electric shock treatment (1938) for manic and depressive patients
    d) The appearance of psychotropic drugs (1952)
    e) Extensive use of prefrontal lobotomy (investigated by Kostic, 1953). Egaz Moniz in 1955 won the Nobel Prize for his work in this field.

The possibility of introducing actual treatment and conrol into three major areas of psychiatric illness encouraged general optimism. Wagner-Jauregg's accidental discovery of the positive therapeutic effects of malaria infection in treating psychotic patients (1877), first tested in 1917 and later adapted to the heat treatment, raised hopes that his success might be duplicated in all areas of psychopathology. Thanks to Sakel's masterstroke, the prognosis of schizophrenia reversed itself and became hopeful instead of poor. Before he developed the pharmacological shock treatment, 4 out of 5 schizophrenia sufferers remained in hospitals. Now only 1 out of 5 is considered unable to respond to treatment. There is no question that Sakel's work has been the inspiration for the active attack on schizophrenia in tens of thousands of cases. The use of convulsant drugs and electric shocks as therapeutic measures in severe psychoneuroses, though it recalls the icy plunge and the snake pit condemned by Pinel, gave new impetus to the biochemical approach to mental disorders which dominates the field today. Both the removal of neural tissue (lobectomy) and severance of fibers (lobotomy) have helped sufferers from severe psychiatric illness. Kostic studied 339 leucotomized patients and found that prefrontal lobotomy produces equally good results in different forms of schizophrenia and in cases of psychoneurosis.

2) *Interest in the nature and treatment of mental illness* has been awakened. Thanks to great humanitarians and psychiatrists like Clifford Beers, Sigmund Freud, Alfred Adler, Carl Gustav Jung, Harry Stack Sullivan, Karen Horney, and Adolph Meyer, the attitude toward the patient and his emotional problems has changed. He is no longer rejected as "hopeless and disgusting" by his family and society; he is accepted and treated with loving kindness. The general public is becoming aware of its responsibility toward the mentally ill.

3) We now realize that *custodial mental hospitals must be transformed into active treatment areas.* Psychiatrists, sociologists, and psychologists alike recognize the importance of active treatment areas in caring for the mentally ill. The transfer of patients who do not need to be in secluded areas or who are adversely affected by isolation and the establishment of well-organized community clinics or psychiatric wards in general hospitals are major factors in the re-education of the psychiatric profession and the general public. Three factors have contributed to the trend toward the spread of active treatment areas:

    a) Maxwell Jones' "Therapeutic Community" and the recent conference on therapeutic communities in Manhattan State Hospital (1959).

    b) Studies of custodial versus therapeutic psychiatric hospitals by Stanton and Schwartz, Greenblatt and

Levinson, Wilmer, Caudill and Belknap.

c) Ackerman's studies of the psychodynamics of family life.

The trend away from strictly custodian care of mental patients and the positive approach that has been evolving since 1917 are reflected in Hoch's "Open Door Policy" and in Kris' studies of the effect of psychiatric after care clinics. The future course of psychiatry is charted in *Action for Mental Health,* the official report of Senator Hill, Kenneth Appel and a group of fifty leading psychiatric and neurological associations. William E. Lawrence sums it up in the science column of the New York *Times* (March 26, 1961) and calls attention to the main areas in which improvements are needed:

1) Elaborate basic research is needed to determine the causes of schizophrenia, manic-depressive psychosis, and many other forms of mental illness. These studies must be carried out in the laboratory, the hospital, and the community clinic.
2) Since 80 out of 100 mental patients in the U.S. are still kept under elementary custodial conditions, funds must be made available for constructing smaller clinics, cottages and psychiatric wards in general hospitals with good teaching facilities.
3) Simple psychotherapeutic work should be done by trained psychologists and social workers. Major problems in patient and family counseling should be handled by the more highly trained psychiatrist, neurologist and psychoanalyst.

H. PETER LAQUEUR, M.D.

NAME INDEX

Ackerman, 160
Adler, 159
Alzheimer, 124
Amelung, 15, 65, 91, 92
Appel, 160
Arnold, 25, 44, 47, 122
Autenrieth, 15, 25-26, 33, 53, 70, 74, 81, 85-86, 100, 140
Bayle, 123
Beers, 159
Belknap, 160
Beneke, 25
Bergman, 53, 124, 126
Bini, 158
Bird, 44, 63, 113
Blumröder, 17, 30, 44, 47, 50, 58, 113, 122, 126
Boerhave, 19
Broca, 127
Brodmann, 129
Burdach, 28
Burrows, 38
Buzorini, 55
Calmeil, 123
Caudill, 160
Celsus, 88
Cerletti, 158
Charcot, 132
Charlesworth, 136
Chiarugi, 25, 42-43, 51, 54, 61, 63, 72, 82, 89, 90, 112, 114, 123-124
Condillac, 27
Conolly, 14, 19, 21, 70, 136, 139-140
Cox, 43, 48, 58, 67-68, 72, 85, 87-88, 120, 122
Crichton, 25, 44
Cullen, 16, 25
Dahl, 105
Damerow, 23, 28, 30, 56, 73, 90, 104, 144

Daquin, 25, 27
Darwin, 87
Davis, 23
DeBoismont, 143
Diem, 133
Eglfing, 148
Ennemoser, 107
Erhard, 79
Eschenmayer, 53
Esquirol, 11, 18-19, 24-25, 51-52, 54, 62, 74, 81, 97, 114, 116-118, 122-123, 135
Ferrus, 145
Feuerstein, 32
Flechsing, 127
Flemming, 54, 113
Fleury, 135
Flourens, 127
Frank, 11, 15, 103
Freud, 159
Friedrich, 19, 25, 42, 113
Fries, 25
Fritsch, 127
Fürstner, 120
Gall, 68, 122, 126-127
Georget, 81
Glaser, 125
Glauber, 82
Grashey, 120
Greding, 122
Greenblatt, 159
Gregory, 96
Griesinger, 23, 111, 113, 115-116, 120, 132, 148
Grohman, 28
Groos, 17, 37, 55
Gudden, 115, 121, 124, 148
Guislain, 45, 47, 51-52, 56, 58, 61-62, 81, 114-115, 122, 126, 142
Gummi, 144
Guntz, 14

161

Hagen, 115
Haindorf, 51, 68, 73, 76, 81, 98, 100, 107, 108, 113, 120, 126
Hale, 47
Hallaran, 88
Hardenberg, 106, 152
Haslam, 16, 25, 74
Hayner, 13, 15, 25, 80, 89, 91-92
Hegel, 32
Heil, 113
Heilbronner, 141
Heinroth, 17, 25, 29, 33-39, 41-46, 50, 55-56, 63, 68, 71, 74, 76, 79, 82, 85, 88, 97-98, 103, 107, 112-113, 138, 140
Heyner, 68
Hill, 136, 160
Hippocrates, 41
Hirsch, 79
Hitzig, 120, 127
Hoch, 11, 160
Hoffbauer, 25, 48, 71, 73
Hogarth, 18
Hoppe, 141
Horn, 15, 17-18, 25, 46, 48, 61, 64, 85-86, 88, 97, 104, 112
Horney, 159
Ideler, 28, 46, 113
Jacobi, 17, 27, 42-43, 46, 55, 65, 67, 72, 97-98, 105, 111, 113, 115, 122-123
Jankendorf, 106
Jones, 159
Jung, 159
Kahlbaum, 116-117
Kant, 20, 25, 27-28, 32, 55
Kerner, 53
Kieser, 30, 32, 113
Knight, 88, 91, 123
Kocher, 131
Koppe, 145
Kostic, 158-159
Kris, 160
Lahr, 99, 135
Laneisi, 125
Langer, 20-21
Langermann, 15, 64, 70, 97

Larochefoucault-Lianfourt, 21
Lawrence, 160
Leupoldt, 92, 97, 108, 112
Leuret, 136
Levinson, 160
Lichtenberg, 14
Liebreich, 143
Liepmann, 120
Linnaeus, 54
Locke, 27
Lorry, 25
Ludwig, 149
MacBride, 16
Magnan, 133
Mahir, 12, 18, 56, 61
Marcus, 112
Mass, 113
Marshal, 44
Mayo, 120
Meckel, 120
Meduna, 158
Mendel, 134
Meyer, 139, 159
Meynert, 112, 120-121, 129
Mitivie, 67
Möbius, 132
Monakon, 121
Moniz, 158
Monro, 14
Morel, 133
Müller, 13-14, 17, 20-21, 25, 50, 122, 155
Munk, 127
Nasse, 25-26, 42
Neisser, 142
Neumann, 15-16, 32, 47, 58-59, 62, 69-70, 80, 82, 86, 98, 113, 120, 123, 125
Nissl, 121, 124
Nostiz, 85, 89, 102, 106, 112, 150
Obersteiner, 121
Oegg, 16, 51, 55, 58, 109
Parchappe, 142
Pargeter, 25, 76
Parry, 62
Perfect, 25

Pienitz, 25, 62, 65
Piloz, 134
Pinel, 20-21, 23, 25, 27, 33, 50, 62, 70, 74, 77, 90, 92, 96, 135, 158
Pitsch, 104
Pravaz, 144
Ramaer, 20
Reil, 10, 14, 20, 25, 27, 33, 42, 45, 56, 69, 71, 78, 89, 92, 95-96, 102, 104, 107, 122, 145
Richard, 63, 80
Riedl, 56
Roller, 17, 26, 76, 82, 91, 98
Rudin, 134
Ruer, 107
Ruhland, 27
Rush, 17, 43, 47, 50, 52, 62, 64, 76, 81, 97, 120
Sakel, 158
Sandtmann, 46
Schellhammer, 125
Schneider, 56, 58-62, 64, 67-68, 73, 85, 98
Scholz, 143
Schwartz, 159

Sieburg, 107
Snell, 115
Solbrig, 112, 148
Sonnenstein, 78, 89
Spurzheim, 126
Stanton, 159
Sullivan, 159
Tissot, 51
Tuke, 12, 67
Van Swieten, 19
Vering, 50, 59, 63, 71, 77, 100, 113, 123
Vocke, 151, 154
Voigt, 129
Wagner-Jauregg, 158
Walther, 32
Wassermann, 130
Wattenberg, 141
Weigert, 124
Wernicke, 112, 120-121, 127, 129
Westphal, 115, 120
Willis, 16-17, 42, 70, 74, 76, 81, 97, 125
Wilmer, 160
Wolff, 120
Zeller, 51, 56, 98, 115, 123

Lightning Source UK Ltd.
Milton Keynes UK
UKOW07f1309291215

265483UK00001B/101/P